D1460480

The Better Land

in Search of the Lost Boy Sopranos

Stephen R. Beet

Published by
Rectory Press
Portlaw, Co. Waterford, Ireland
Tel/Fax: 051 387888
rectorypress@eircom.net

ISBN: 1-903698-14-6

Cover picture:
The Choristers of The Temple Church, at Angmering,
Surrey, 1926. Ernest Lough, Ronald Mallett (2nd and
3rd from left) and E.V. Bartlett (3rd from right)

In Memory of T.E.M. Barber M.A.
Vicar of Spondon, 1939 - 1986

Author's Acknowledgements

It would be impossible to acknowledge everyone who has helped in the preparation of this book. Several have been mentioned in the text and I hope that they will accept my sincere thanks. However, I should also like to thank the following:

Peter Purves, for his excellent and enlightening *Foreword*.

Edward Power, my editor and publisher, for his vision and expertise, in recognising the book's potential.

Eve Barsham, who reviewed and corrected the manuscript.

Colin Charnley, Douglas Carrington, and Brian Pearson for providing much factual information and invaluable advice.

Frederick Appleby, and Martin Carson, who scanned many of the photographs.

David Lewer, in addition to giving invaluable help in preparing the chapter about the soloists of the Temple Church, provided and identified the photographs for that section.

Timothy Day at the National Sound Archives, Sonita Cox at EMI, and Hazel Simpson at the BBC Written Archives, also helped in checking factual information.

The Dean and Chapter of Manchester Cathedral, for kindly giving permission to quote from the Chapter records.

The help of the editors of several newspapers and magazines must also be acknowledged, In addition to those already named, Philip Titcombe of *Choir Schools Today*, Clare Stevens of *Choir and Organ*, Antonia Couling of *The Singer,* Tully Potter of International Classical Record Collector, Bob Crooks at BBC Ulster and Eddie McIlwaine at *The Belfast Telegraph*, have all publicised the book and have been instrumental in helping to trace many of the artistes featured.

I should like to pay tribute to the music teachers, choir

trainers and parents of the boys featured in this book. Most choirmasters and managers were true mentors and friends to their pupils though others were less so, and there were instances of exploitation. But we must not necessarily judge yesterday's behaviour by today's standards.

Were it not for the vision of the smaller gramophone companies, several artistes would never have been recorded. The British Brunswick and Vocalion labels fell victim to the depressed economic conditions of the 1920s. It is fortunate that the voices of so many boys have been preserved for posterity.

Contents

Temple Church, London

Foreword

When Stephen Beet first contacted me, it was in rela-
tion to some sleeve notes he wanted to accompany
one of the newly-mastered Better Land CD's that he
was about to produce, and which included some remastered, and previously almost unheard tracks of
my father, Kenneth Purves. I must confess that I was
really unable to offer him much information. My
knowledge of my dad as a boy soprano was small and
sketchy, and based on family hearsay rather than any
substantial fact. However, it was a pleasant request to
have received because, apart from hearing the tracks
on the original discs, made in 1927, and very dam-
aged, I had never heard my dad as a boy soprano. I
didn't even have a copy of the records. However, my
Uncle Alan, Ken's eldest brother, had kept a set which
had ended up in the keeping of my cousin, David.
Most were in poor condition, though some still
played.

I had always known Ken had been a celebrity
of sorts, because my grandmother had shown me the
certificates he had received for being best Boy Soloist,
three years in succession, at the Blackpool Music
Festival – a then-unprecedented feat. I had always
known that he had developed a fine bass singing
voice, and he and his brother Douglas (a good baritone) would often entertain in the evenings at
Christmas and other festive times. But that was about
as far as it went. To receive, via Stephen, a letter in
Ken's own hand describing his years as a boy soprano
of some renown, his broadcasting on the BBC, and his

touring the country performing before concert crowds (2000 and more), was an absolute joy.

My dad, being a modest man, had never talked about these days to me, nor, strangely enough, had my grandmother. To read that one of his records, for which he had never received any royalties, sold over 330,000 copies, was astonishing. Even today, many a modern performer who would give anything to achieve this level of success. There was one thing that the family did seem generally agreed upon: they all firmly believed that the world-famous Ernest Lough recording of *O for the Wings of a Dove*, played continually on the radio, was actually my dad's recording. A nice vanity but, having heard both recordings - my dad's wonderfully restored considering the state of the originals - it is quite obvious that they were wrong.

The Lough recording is so beautifully pure, every note finely sung; and, whilst my dad's is, to my mind, a more dramatically-sung solo, it lacks just a little in finesse. Some will prefer one over the other, and there is no question but that each is excellent in its own way. But Master Lough deserved his worldwide recognition.

It is a shame that many excellent boy sopranos do not go on to great things once their voices break. In my father's case it was ill-health that meant he was unable to face the rigours of a professional performing life. He was diagnosed with diabetes at the age of 13, and was lucky to survive to even take part at Blackpool, let alone go on to adulthood, marriage, fatherhood and, ultimately, to live to a good old 75 years of age.

My thanks go to Douglas Carrington who traced him living in Swanage, Dorset, in 1985, shortly before his death, which means that I, my son, and my grandson, and our families can each thrill to the sound of his beautiful voice. In spite of the fact that we were in regular contact, my dad, modest to the end, never told me of the meeting or of his conversations with Douglas. I only wish that he had survived long enough to hear the re-mastered recordings.

My own singing career was nothing like as spectacular. I was a regular soloist as a soprano at school, but my voice broke quite early, just turned 14, and I developed into an averagely-good tenor. I appeared in several shows which required me to sing, and at college in the late '50's I was the singer in a skif-fle/rock band. My first professional job in London was as top tenor in the chorus at the London Palla-dium, and I sang once or twice in TV shows and pan-tomimes, but singing was never of prime importance in my life.

Stephen Beet has written an excellent and remarkable book to complement the excellent and remarkable series of CD's featuring the greatest of the boy sopranos in full voice. There are so many lovely stories of success. Iwan Davies, Denis Wright, Derek Barsham, and Billy Neely, are among those whose lives are recounted in the narrative of THE BETTER LAND. It is a noble title. The Lost Boy Sopranos have been found again and given a little immortality.

Peter Purves.
Suffolk, January 2005.

Introduction

The set of six CD's, *The Better Land - Great Boy Sopranos*, is a series which was begun in 1999 and features the recorded voices of some of the boy sopranos of the twentieth century. The booklet with each disc contains, as far as it has been possible to provide, a brief account of the singing career of the boys included, together with the limited selection of photographs available to us at the time of production. The series does not claim to be comprehensive, nor does it include the recordings of every single boy soprano brought to the microphone. We have aimed, however, to include some of the best material recorded during the first half of the century.

We have been concerned to use only those discs which are in a good state of preservation. During the last five years more discs have come to light and, as far as possible, we have sought to use those depending on quality. All the recordings feature boys trained in traditional 'head tone' methods, and much modern material has been rejected as not compatible with the 'atmosphere' of the series, though more recent material has been included if it meets the stated criteria.

One of the aims of the research has been to trace either the 'boys' themselves or their descendants: since the issue of Volume 1 in the autumn of 1999 it has been possible to do this in most cases and I must record my thanks to Trevor Ford of the Royal School of Church Music who had the faith and vision to agree that it would be of great interest to musicians and the general public alike to make available for the first time on CD the voices of these boy sopranos who for a brief space of time enjoyed fame, and sometime fortune, before disappearing seemingly for ever into oblivion. Trevor put me in contact with Martin Monkman, the proprietor of *Amphion Recordings* to whom I am greatly indebted, and without his help the project would not have been realised.

Glyn Paflin of *The Church Times*, Peter Worsley of *Evergreen* magazine, and Eddie McIlwaine of *The Belfast Telegraph*, have given me enormous help in tracing many of the 'lost boys'. Others have been discovered by accident: for instance Peter Ward, the nephew of John Bonner, happened to see his uncle's name on the front cover of Volume 1 when he was wandering around a record shop!

Some of the biographical information contained in the CD booklets is incomplete and now somewhat out of date. Hence I have attempted here to detail the careers of these boys who, so long ago, set their voices forever in hot wax. Although this book may be of interest to social historians, it does not claim to be either a definitive history of the subject or an academic work. The story is really *my* search for the 'lost boy sopranos' and as a result must needs be a somewhat subjective account, drawing on both factual information and the recollections of the 'boys' themselves.

On the advice of my publisher and others I have resisted the temptation to include a detailed discussion on voice production and training methods used by choirmasters in the first half of the twentieth century. These matters are of more specialist interest and may well be the subject of a later book.

Many of the boys featured were members of choirs and I have had to exclude the histories of these choirs from the narrative except when the story of an individual or group of soloists is bound up with the choir to which he or they belonged. Thus, the histories of both the *Martin Boys' Choir* and *The Temple Church Choir* are included in some detail. Others may well form the basis of later study.

Each chapter aims to tell the story of an individual boy's singing career, sketching other details in brief. Emphasis has been placed on the unusual and as far as possible conjecture has been avoided, every attempt being made to substantiate the facts. I have always written with the full co-operation and permission of the artiste or his representative. I have tried to present a continuous narrative which would be of interest to the general reader and with this in mind the first four chapters form an almost contnous and chronological story taking us from the late1920s right up to 1960. Each boy's career ended more or less as the next boy came to fame.

It was sometimes convenient to group several boys together under one heading for reasons that will become obvious to the reader. The final chapters mention the boys of whom we as yet know little, in the hope that information may come to light in the future. I hope that what we relate may not just be confined to the pages of history but be an inspiration to those with the vision and ability to effect a renaissance.

The Better Land

Iwan Davies

The Little Welsh Minstrel

Iwan Davies

He sang before the King and Queen at a private Command Performance, and twice toured Canada and the United States, once as a solo artiste. He was many times broadcast by the BBC and recorded by two record companies. The story of boy soprano Iwan Davies, who was known as 'The Little Welsh Minstrel', is remarkable even when told alongside those of the other boys featured in this book.

Arthur Iwan Davies was born the youngest of four brothers in February 1916. His father was a merchant who kept a general stores at Pantteg Cross, near Llandyssul, Cardiganshire. Few people knew anything about Iwan until I discovered a flickering film-clip in the Pathé archives of this boy soprano, who, it was reported, had shot to fame in 1932 after being commanded to perform before King George V and Queen Mary. Unfortunately, due to the use of nitrate-based film, the soundtrack had completely dis-integrated leaving Iwan singing silently at the piano. The credits told us he was a chorister at The London Choir School, Denmark Hill, but all that survived of Iwan's career were a handful of records featuring his distinctive 'full-toned' voice, reminiscent of a bygone age. I selected his recording of Stephen Adams' *The Holy City* for inclusion on *The Better Land* series of CDs and became determined to find out more.

Following an appeal in *The Church Times,* I was contacted by the widow of a childhood friend of Davies, Helen Jones of Denbigh. Mrs Jones told me that Iwan had moved to Winchester where he habeen the manager of Woolworth's. I had no further clues to work on, so I visited Winchester to seek out any staff who might have remembered him. Unfortunately, the store had been closed for several years. As a last resort, I went into the offices of *The Hampshire Chronicle* where by good fortune I happened to speak to Kit Neilson, the same reporter who had covered Iwan's retirement party twenty-five years previously. He told me that Iwan had died in January 1996, but that his daughter-in-law was living in the area.

By the age of thirteen, Iwan was well-known as a boy soprano. He had been 'discovered' by Professor Ted Morgan, of Cardiff University, when singing, aged eight, at a 'little social party. He had won his first cup at the age of six and was to go on to win an incredible 52 cups and well over 300 prizes during his career.

Various reports and reviews of his singing praise his ability and stage presence. He was always received with thunderous applause, especially after the ever-popular ballad *Daddy* by Lemon - Behrend, with which he was particularly associated.

A review, probably dating from Christmas 1928, seemed to augur well for the future by remarking that 'his breath control, interpretative gifts and platform style were astonishing for one of his age.'

Iwan Davies is thirteen when we are able to take up the story recorded in his scrapbook in detail. We begin in his own words, written a few years later.

'My first real success as a vocalist was attained when I won the Boys' Solo competition at the National Eisteddfod of Wales at Liverpool in August 1929. Immediately after this, I was given the opportunity to broadcast for the first time.' The music critic of the local paper was particularly impressed by Iwan's and his fellow competitors' performances at the Eisteddfod:

'The sheer platform accomplishment of these fine singers was staggering. They have all the arts, tricks and mannerisms of your hardened professional. The test pieces, too, were no easy matter. Boys under sixteen were required to sing the florid air *O had I*

Jubal's Lyre from Handel's *Joshua*.   The marvel is not that they sang some of the runs out of tune, but that they sang them at all.   Well might the winner be con-gratulated on his breath control.   What assurance, what terrific aplomb these young men displayed!'

Iwan had been educated at Capel Cynon and Llandyssul County Schools. When he was fourteen he won a four years' scholarship at the recently formed London Choir School: a report suggests he was the first amongst the six candidates selected, and also the first Welsh boy to be admitted. The school (first listed as such in the 1926 Trades' Directory) was at the top of Dog Kennel Hill in the London district of Denmark Hill, and was founded by Carlton Borrow for the express purpose of providing choristers and soloists for some of the best churches and chapels in London.

Iwan had already sung at the Central Hall Westminster in 1929, but his professional career in London really began in September 1930 when he became a pupil at the school. He had been there but a day when he was called upon to sing solo at a memo-rial service. The very next Sunday he was singing before His Royal Highness the Prince of Wales at All Saints Church, Westminster and he then became a chorister in the Savoy Chapel.

This Royal Chapel, situated near the Strand in central London, had been founded in 1246 and rebuilt in 1524. In 1374 'the little clerks' were paid 40 shillings apiece per annum. Shortly after, in 1381, John O' Gaunt's regal Savoy Palace was destroyed by Wat Tyler's Kentish rebels during the Peasants' Revolt. When the chapel was restored by order of the will of Henry V11, red and gold costumes and Tudor ruffs were introduced for the children.

A few weeks after Iwan (now fifteen) had joined the choir the boys were invited by Montreal agent, Ernest Desaules to undertake a four-month, all-expenses-paid tour of Canada. The other choristers were D.F. Beard (13), A. Vann (13), C. Meek (12), F.T. Moore (11), N. Boulton (13), E.W. Golds (13), R.S. Haddock (10), A.J. Fowle (11), R.L. Betts (13), J.C. Beynon (13), and S.W. Bennett (14).

The boys sailed to Canada on the S.S. Laurentic in October 1930. It was the first time in 700 years that the choir had left England and this was one of the first major tours undertaken by any English cathedral or chapel choir in the world (though the lay-clerks of St. George's Chapel, Windsor Castle together with the choristers of Westminster Abbey had toured Canada in 1927). The press coverage of the event was extensive, showering the boys with a level of publicity almost unknown in those days and more akin to that afforded film and pop stars in today's world. During the passage it seems that the boys continued with their lessons and gave several concerts, much to the appreciation of fellow passengers. As the ship docked in Montreal, the press were waiting for them and followed their every move for the next six months.

The boys made their debut in St Andrew's Church, Sherbrooke. They then embarked on a three week concert tour of the Maritime Provinces, before returning to Montreal in November accompanied throughout by Carlton Borrow, the sub-organist of the Savoy Chapel. The Canadian pianist, Matthew Heft, compèred the programmes and performed solo items on the piano. The choir's business manager, Ernest Desaules, was the only other adult to undertake the tour.

This 'coast-to-coast' was soon to be extended by two months. From the outset, Iwan was the principal solo attraction, sometimes singing as many as five items during a performance. It was the custom of the choir that the soloists remain anonymous but for some reason Iwan was the only boy allowed to be mentioned by name in programmes. At a matinée performance put on especially for children, in the Toronto Massey Hall, he was greeted with great excitement as he stepped forward to take each solo. At Picton his singing 'brought moisture to many eyes.'

The choir then toured and gave concerts in all the principal cities of Canada and some of the largest cities of the USA. *The Calgary Herald* reported that 'a dozen rosy-cheeked little lads arrived at 1.50pm and rested at the Palliser Hotel before undertaking their concert programme. Every boy was a soloist, even ten-year-old Master R.S. Haddock.'

'Boys,' the report goes on, 'have an advantage over all others in the ease with which they can take the highest notes. The penetrating quality of these boys' voices is remarkable'

The concerts invariably comprised two halves – one religious, for which the boys were vested in their scarlet cassocks, ruffs and surplices; and the other secular, when the boys cast off their mediaeval glory and changed into Eton suits. At his debut in Sherbrooke, Iwan was received with great enthusiasm: 'Canada seldom hears a boy capable of such singing.'

But it wasn't just Iwan who impressed the vast audiences. The whole choir excited the most extreme praise. The boys 'caught something of the spirit of a faith that has come down through the ages.' Iwan noted in the margin of his programme that the audience was 'so enthusiastic [they] nearly brought the roof in!' The Orpheum Theatre in Prince Albert was packed to capacity for the concert arranged by the St. Alban's Cathedral Choir. The choir must have looked a grand sight appearing on the otherwise unadorned stage.

'The boys came out in scarlet cassocks and white surplices followed by their director, Carlton Borrow, who seated himself behind a screen of palms at the piano behind them. They sang, hands behind their backs, with no self-consciousness... They brought the traditional music of the English Church and interpreted it delightfully, with such perfect articulation and much spiritualit... To have heard the singing of the children of the Chapel of the Savoy is to have partaken of a benediction. Iwan Davies will be remembered [because] in addition to his beautiful voice he possesses that illusive characteristic called "platform presence" and a faculty for losing himself in the spirit of the song. The purity of this boy's voice is amazing.'

Just one reporter thought it rather inappropriate for the boys to be singing robed before footlights but added that 'the simplicity of the stage arrangements was admirably contrived and nothing could have been more sedate, or less self-conscious than the demeanor of the boys themselves.'

The choir was praised for catering for all tastes and it was much appreciated that the second half of each programme should always be secular. One critic was rather amused by this, remarking that 'while the boys here discarded cassocks, they never quite came out of chapel.'

All the boys had solos from time to time but most of the time these were sung by Iwan. However, little Master Haddock also won the hearts of the audience: on one occasion *A Night Nursery* by Arundale was sung by the choir's "baby", who could not be named on the programme. 'It seems a shame that the name of the lad was not allowed publicity, but it is the rule of the choir.   Even an encore was denied him [for] although the audience [had] insisted, the "baby" .... bowed to discipline.'

At the close of each concert *God Save the King* was sung, always 'as we have never heard it, softly, reverently, loyally.'

Throughout the tour the press reports continued to be ecstatic, the only reservations being about the suitability of some of the more sentimental pieces in the second half of the programmes.

The boys travelled extensively by train and crossed the continent several times. One might ask what became of their school work, but it seems that 'reading, 'riting and 'rithmetic' were conducted during the long train journeys, much to the amusement of the press who liked to quiz the boys about their morning lessons!   Towards the end of the tour the boys were thrilled to travel in an aeroplane piloted by two wartime Aces.   Asked if they were frightened, one lad replied: 'Oh no, sir. The world looked like a map.' 'Surrounded by mountains,' added another.

The journey was undertaken to give a series of concerts in Edmonton. The choir boarded two Canada Airways Fokker monoplanes at Saskatoon, the two aeroplanes travelling side by side as they winged over the prairie land and on to the city of Edmonton. After landing, the boys were keen to point out that the customary in-transit lesson had been cancelled that morning for obvious reasons. Reporters clamoured round the planes noting the boys' rather over-dressed state, 'dressed for the kind of weather which England expects Canada to have.' Each boy had overshoes and a heavy blue overcoat. They stepped briskly out of their machines, looked around, and were greeted by a crowd of about 250 people who congregated on the airfield for a glimpse of them.

'They made a picturesque group as they stood in the shadow of the aeroplane's wing in the bright afternoon sunshine, each of the twelve with his red cassock rolled neatly under his arm, and the long red tassel swinging gayly (sic) from his "mortar-board". The typical Alberta sunshine seemed to render the heavy snow shoes unnecessary, but no chances were being taken in keeping the boys in perfect health.'

Asked if they were keen to go home, the boys replied a definite 'No!' As they left the field to fulfil their matinée performance for the Edmonton children, no-one would credit the pranks they were reported to have been up to in Toronto and Kitchener – the round chubby one especially - as having a grain of truth.

Sadly the extended tour, which had lasted six months, came to an end with a rather poorly attended farewell concert in Montreal, a city in which they had given several concerts throughout the winter.   In fact, the press, severely criticised the concert-going public for missing one of the finest performances of the whole tour in His Majesty's Theatre.

'The choir was treated rather badly by the musical public .... for the audience which assembled in the theatre scarcely numbered more than a handful of people. This was particularly unfortunate inso-much as the boys sang a far superior programme than they gave at previous appearances in the city. Also they appeared to be in better form than before, singing with considerably more finish and style.   The training of this choir has evidently been a very thorough one along certain lines. The tone the boys produce is good, the enunciation of the words and the sense of rhythm they possess, better.   It is possible to catch every syl-lable of the lines of their songs and choruses, a rare enough thing even in an adult choir.'

And so towards the end of April 1931 it was

time for the boys to return to England. They boarded the Red Star Line, Triple Screw *S.S. Pennland*, where it seemed they dined in fine style on dishes as varied as oysters on half shell, Spanish olives, smoked beef, poached shad back, loin of veal, and salami of celery fed duckling. If the boys felt a little flat at the prospect of returning home to the daily round of lessons at the school, and services at the Savoy Chapel, little could Iwan have known the kind of reception awaiting him upon his return from his 'whistle-stop' tour. For a boy soprano to have achieved so much was quite remarkable in itself, but the events which were to unfold over the next twelve months were just as astonishing.

Back in his native Wales, Iwan was honoured by the people of his home town, Llandyssul, where the whole community seems to have turned out to greet him. A lavish celebration was laid on and the proceedings opened with a sumptuous tea presided over by the local Member of Parliament, Mr H. Morris. Several local magistrates and everyone who was anyone for miles around seemed to have been attendance. Iwan's former teacher, Professor Ted Morgan, of Pontwelly, was also present. There was a huge iced cake bearing the inscription 'Croesaw nol i Wan' (Welcome Home to Iwan). After tea everyone adjourned to the chapel where the Reverend Tom Davies expressed his heartfelt delight. He urged Iwan that whatever lay in store for him he should never 'forget his native hearth'.

The story now moves forward almost a year in time. Iwan left the Chapel of The Savoy and was transferred to the popular church of All Souls, Langham Place, next to Broadcasting House, which had just been completed but was not yet in use.

At this point a 'Royal Command' to sing before His Majesty came via Sir Hill Child, Deputy

Master of the Household in a cable to the boy, who was now staying in London with the Curate of All Souls. Iwan and his accompanist Ted Morgan arrived at Buckingham Palace on St. David's Day, 1932. They had spent the previous three days carefully selecting five songs to be performed in the White Drawing Room, and it was there they were received. They spent the next two hours at the palace, and more than an hour with the King and Queen, singing over a dozen songs! Seated with the King and Queen were many ladies and gentlemen of the Royal Household and suspended from the ceiling in the centre of the room was a massive glass chandelier. Iwan took his place beside the white grand piano and began to sing. Everything went as expected until the end of his first song. Then events took a course of their own. It was soon evident that Iwan would have to supplement his chosen programme, as the Queen requested some of her own favourites, including *Jesu, Lover of my Soul*.

In addition to the Queen's requests, Iwan sang his five prepared songs including Handel's *O had I Jubal's lyre*, which he was later to record. 'The Queen wanted to hear *Land of my Fathers,* and I was very glad when asked to sing it in Welsh. The royal couple both shook hands with me after I had finished. Then, to my astonishment, they gave me a lovely silver pencil with the Royal Arms and the initials 'GMR'. I shall treasure it all my life.'

Iwan left the palace and was greeted by a host of reporters who quizzed him closely about his experience. He explained to them that he had not after all been nervous and reminded them that he had lost all his shyness on his recent Canadian tour, singing to vast crowds sometimes numbering 16,000 people! Iwan returned to school to face a hectic week indeed. The next day the press were at the door asking to pho-

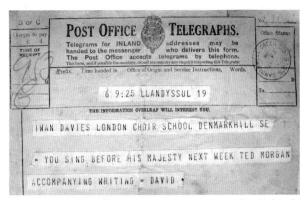

tograph him at lessons and at practice. The telephone bell rang constantly and there was a steady stream of callers asking if he could accept private engagements. Music publishers invited him to promote their latest song. To say (in the words of *The Pathé Gazette*) that he 'shot to fame overnight' was no exaggeration. In the course of a week he had been filmed by the news-reel, offered two more broadcasts, and was recorded by HMV on 4th March. Everything, it seems, was done in a hurry as it was feared his voice must soon be rested. By the end of the week he was offered and had accepted three engagements.

There were to be two twenty minute broad-casts from Savoy Hill for which he would be paid twenty guineas. In addition, *The Daily Mail* reported that the famous tenor John McCormack was keen to see him regarding his future career. However, the Choir School was more than a little anxious about Iwan's success, particularly when he was invited to sign a contract to sing at The Trocadero cabaret in Shaftesbury Avenue for a weekly fee of £25.

An official of the school told *The Daily Mail* that Iwan's voice was exceptional since it had not broken yet but it was not likely that it could last much longer. 'The terms of his scholarship here would prevent him from accepting such engagements as that offered by the restaurant.' However, when pressed by the reporter it was admitted that they could do little to stop him as the boy could be withdrawn from the school without notice.

Despite the prohibition, Iwan did accept the offer to sing at The Trocadero. As he was a minor, the Reverend Oswald Brenton, acting as his guardian, signed on his behalf and the contract was ceremonially presented to Iwan, who was dressed in his robes in All Souls Church in front of a host of newspaper photographers.

It is not clear for how long Iwan sang at The Trocadero, although reports seem to indicate that it was a matter of a week or two at the most. Reporters who caught up with him at the rehearsal described the scene:

'Around him were sounds of busy preparations for his cabaret debut. Waiters rushed here and there, instruments were being tuned in readiness, programmes were being discussed and Master Davies was quite unmoved, save for a little gleam in his eye- that he could not quite subdue.'

In March 1932, Iwan's father in Wales received a telegram from Decca:

WILL OFFER £50 5% ADVANCE ROYALTY
FOUR TITLES STOP WILL PHONE 10 AM FRIDAY STOP
MAGNIFICENT PUBLICITY OFFERED

One of the four songs recorded was Stephen Adams' *The Holy City* featured in *The Better Land* series. It was advertised as the 'Amazing Record of *The Holy City* by the Royal Command Boy Soprano'. A few days later, Iwan was once again at the BBC singing in The National Programme. His days as a boy soprano were not yet at an end and he was to continue singing for another full year.

Far from resting his voice, Iwan immediately embarked on a major tour of his native Wales with Professor Morgan as his accompanist. Just two of the venues were the Central Hall, Clydach Vale, where he was repeatedly encored, and in a hall in Rhos, where he 'gave a perfect display of beautiful phrasing and carefully produced notes.'

Wherever he appeared in the Principality, Iwan was showered with praise. The public thronged every hall and theatre expectantly and were always thrilled by his performance. At Aberystwyth on June 10th he appeared on stage four times during the course of the concert. At Colwyn Bay, where he appeared for the first time, he 'more than exceeded expectations [and] sang so beautifully and effectively that the audience could scarcely contain itself in the admiration of the wonderful lad. Here, his 'rich and mellow voice of great compass' was praised after performing such songs as Emett Adams' *God send you back to me*, and *The Holy City*. At every concert the audience called for encores, so much so that at the Pavilion, Caernarvon, there was a call for calm and order after the audience wanted to hear him again. The conductor had to appeal to them not to be so pressing. Finally Iwan was brought out to lead the congregation in *Land of My Fathers* and *God Save the King*.

Another correspondent wrote of the same event: 'He came to Caernarvon with a reputation. He had captured the hearts of the music-loving people of the metropolis [and] has been acclaimed as the greatest of boy sopranos. He contributed eight or nine songs; the silvery notes soared sweetly and melodiously, and were heard in every corner of the great building. Iwan Davies came and sang and conquered.

Speculation was rife as to what Iwan would do after his voice had broken. He seemed torn between pursuing a career in music, hoping to train in Italy, or alternativately going into his father's business. Perhaps he knew better than most that having a fine boy soprano voice was no guarantee of a future adult voice worthy of merit. It was common belief in those-days that the longer a boy went on singing after the natural break in the voice, the slimmer the chance of his becoming a fine tenor or baritone. Complete rest was advised for upwards of four or five years.

Had Iwan's album of cuttings and photo-graphs finished at this point one would have assumed that his return to London would have coincided with his retirement as a boy soprano. Not a bit of it! For on New Year's Eve 1932, he set sail on board the Cunard Line *R.M.S. Aurania* to undertake his second Canadian tour. It had been two years since he had undertaken his first tour and now he was approach-ing eighteen years of age.

The passage by all accounts was one of the roughest in memory, and this photograph, taken by Iwan, cap-tured the violence of the waves.

There was little wonder the boat was delayed two days, eventually docking in New York Harbour on 11th January, 1933. Iwan immediately boarded a train and crossed the border into the Dominion, arriving in St John's the following day. He was welcomed 'home' by crowds of well-wishers and greeted by the press.

'I'm making money now to complete my education', he said. 'I expect to go to Italy in a few years'-time to finish off my musical training.'

By train and by aeroplane, Iwan travelled to sing at virtually every important venue in Canada. He did not, however, forget the smaller, out-of-the-way places, once appearing before war veterans gathered in a cold Red Cross Nissen hut. In places such as Montreal, Vancouver, Victoria and Calgary (where he celebrated his eighteenth birthday), huge crowds turned out to see and hear the boy who had won their hearts two years previously. While the lad had grown considerably, it was noted, his voice as was good as ever – better, according to some accounts.

Iwan was as popular with children as he was with adult audiences, dispelling any impression we may have that his appeal was just to a certain generation. In fact, he loved the children's matinees, often allowing the boys and girls to request items from the programme. Asked what he was going to sing for the children at Edmonton, he said: 'I've 46 songs to choose from, so I'll just sing the ones they like the best.' And at St Paul's, Nelson, Iwan sang with a choir of local boys who welcomed him with the Welsh National Anthem.

It seems strange to us that the singing of a boy soprano could cause such excitement across a vast continent. But, in those days, audiences loved to hear boys sing: 'few singers are more beloved than the boy soprano', opined one editorial. Iwan's voice was described as the 'type that appeals [to British and Canadian tastes] strongly. It is the perfect combination of sweet young treble with rich soprano. He is more than a child with a remarkable voice, he is a qualified artiste, capable of being compared favourably with the great singers of his day.'

After Iwan had completed his three-month tour in Victoria, he sailed for home from the Gulf of St. Lawrence, leaving behind him many thousands of admirers. The scrapbook of his boyhood career suddenly breaks off before his return, but with the end of this tour came the inevitable close of his days as a choirboy and soloist. Iwan returned to Wales. His hopes of studying music in Italy seem to have been unfulfilled. Could this have been in some part due to the recent death of his father and the need to look after his mother? He would have been advised to rest his voice for upwards of five years before taking up singing as a baritone. There must have been in his heart a feeling of great sadness that he would perhaps never again in his life reach the dizzy heights that he had achieved as a boy. No matter how good his adult voice might become, he would never again charm an audience in quite the same way.

He joined the firm of F.W. Woolworth's and began work in their Caermarthen store in 1934, and it was here that he began 'the rest of his life', so to speak. But Canada did not forget Iwan and in 1936 the *Vancouver Sun* reported that he was now singing as a baritone.

Iwan would spend the rest of his working life with Woolworth's. By the outbreak of World War Two, he was Assistant Manager of the Swansea store. In February 1940 he was called up and joined the Royal Artillery. In May 1942, he was captured outside

Iwan Davies at Niagara

Tobruk but managed to escape only to be later recaptured, and Vatican Radio soon broadcast that he was in the Benghazi Camp in Italy. While he was in Italian hands, Iwan formed a St. David's Club of 600 members for his fellow prisoners of war.

'They have a choir and a rugby football team, a cricket team, a nigger (sic) minstrel troupe, a cultural class and a debating society,' it was reported. It now seems ironic that Iwan should find himself in Italy, the very country he had set his heart on as a boy.

Iwan was later transferred to Germany, where he continued to arrange concerts for his fellow prisoners. He was liberated by the Americans in 1945 and returned to Llandyssul, which was described as "mad" with joy at his arrival. He was given a rouing reception and the freedom of the town. Following his return, he was to broadcast about his experience of POW life.

Prior to his actual demob, in August 1945, Iwan joined the 'Stars in Battledress Bombshells Army Show,' a group of artistes formed by the War Office for the entertainment of troops in all parts of the country. Many of the members were formerly part of his choir formed during the war. By now he was the principal baritone.

Following demob in 1947, Iwan returned to his job at Woolworth's. A reporter who had interviewed him many years before caught up with him at his home in Bodmin and wrote that '[he is] still the same polite and well-dispositioned Iwan [I met years before]. Sometimes in a nostalgic vein, sometimes in gayer mood, he took his mind back to those days when he sang at the Trocadero for £25 a week. Many are the reminiscences of his two tours of Canada and America'

Iwan's working career took him to Trowbridge and then to Andover. He became manager of Woolworth's Winchester branch, where he remained for fourteen years until his retirement in 1974. At his retirement party, he was presented with remastered copies of his records by Kit Neilson, a young reporter on *The Hampshire Chronicle*, whom I was to contact twenty-five years later.

So Iwan's achievements were not entirely for-gotten. In 1977, he was belatedly elected to the green robed Order of Bards for his distinguished career as a boy soprano following his success at the Liverpool National Eisteddfod in 1929. His late father had also been a member. It was noted by the press that he had had to wait too long for this award.

Arthur Iwan Davies died in January 1996. Sadly, he never lived to see his records appear in *The Better Land* series or to enjoy latter-day recognition he so richly deserved.

Years later, another famous boy soprano was to hail from Wales. But was the career of Aled Jones in the 1980s even remotely as spectacular as that of Iwan Davies forty-five years previously? Before this story was told, one would have been forgiven for thinking that there had been just one famous Welsh boy soprano. Now that it has been told, we can set the record straight and say with confidence that Aled Jones was the most famous Welsh boy soprano of the 20th century *after* Iwan Davies!

I will conclude this chapter with a note on the ships which carried Iwan and his companions across the Atlantic. The *S.S. Laurentic* was a new boat, built by Harland and Wolff in 1927. It went down off the coast of Donegal after being torpedoed in 1940. The *R.M.S. Auriana* (14,000 ton one-funnel passenger liner) wasbuilt by Swan Hunter, Newcastle in 1924. In 1939 she was fitted as an armed merchant cruiser and was torpedoed in 1941, but managed to get back to Rothsay. In 1942 she was sold to the British admiralty, converted to a repair ship and renamed *H.M.S. Artifex*. She was broken up in 1961.

Denis Wright

Denis Wright

I had been working on the task of selecting tracks for a CD of Boys' Voices for some months and *The Last Rose of Summer* sung by Master Denis Wright had been chosen, even though I had no information at all about the boy himself. But in July 1999, following an appeal in *CMQ* (the magazine of The Royal School of Church Music), I received a letter from Fergus Black, a choirmaster in Peterborough informing me that Denis Wright was alive and living near Mansfield. This boy soprano, whose records I had heard played by Richard Baker on the radio programme *These you have Loved* had appeared with many famous artistes, including Alfredo Campoli (violinist), Eileen Joyce, Harriet Cohen, and Solomon (concert pianists), and singers like Owen Brannigan, Florence Austral, Anne Ziegler and Webster Booth, to name but a few. He had broadcast many times, appearing regularly with The Kentucky Minstrels. Moreover, he recorded at HMV with Gerald Moore as accompanist and also appeared with celebrated organists like Reginald Dixon, Robinson Cleaver and Reginald Foort. He also worked with Wee Georgie Wood, Marius Goring, Gillie Potter and Lilian Braithwaite. His most memorable appearance, however, was in The Royal Albert Hall during Henry Wood's 48th promenade concert season, in the first performance of Harry Farjeon's symphonic poem *Pannychis.*

By coincidence, I was born in the same town as Denis Wright and lived my first thirty years eight miles from his front door. But I had been born fifteen years after Denis had made his last record and, as was the case with many of the boys in our story, his discs fell victim to the decision of the BBC no longer to play 78s on Radio 2. I went to see Denis and his wife and played them my proposed CD. 'You haven't included *The Better Land* or *Christopher Robin is saying his prayers*!' said Denis. He gave me a tape of his recordings made with The Kentucky Minstrels in 1942 and it was then that I knew which should be the opening track: *The Better Land* by Hermans - Cowen sums up the mood of the CD and it was destined to become the title of the whole series.

Denis Wright was born in Mansfield on St Swithin's Day 1926. His mother claimed that he cried for 40 days and 40 nights! His father died shortly after he was born, leaving his widow to cope with a large family. Most of the elder brothers and sisters were already in their 'teens or twenties when Denis arrived.

'My sister, Hilda, used the front room of the house as a draper's shop, and when I attended Carter Lane Infants' School at the age of five, I used to take silk stockings for both the Headmistress, Miss Grainger, and my Form Teacher, Miss Flaxton. I believe these cost 11d per pair in old money!

'I noticed that Mr Goodwin, a piano teacher, lived across the road from the school, so one day I called at his house and asked him if he would teach me the piano. He agreed but asked: "Does your mother know about this?" I replied "Oh, yes". "Well," he said, "I had better come and see her!"

'I had not told my mother a thing about my wish to play the piano, so when Mr. Goodwin arrived she was very surprised but she did agree. The lessons cost 1s/3d per fortnight and there were times when mother couldn't afford it, so occasionally I took only one shilling, telling the teacher that she would send the rest the following week, which I don't think she ever did!'

Like many boys of his age, Denis was already a member of his local church choir, but the start of his professional singing career was a direct result of the chance knock on Mr Goodwin's door. The teacher's daughter, Joyce Goodwin (who later became a well-known mezzo-soprano), noticed that Denis had a good voice and asked him to sing for her in a local concert.

At the age of 11 Denis went up to High Oakham Boys' Selective Central School, where the choir, founded in 1927 by the English master, Harry Smith, had already won 120 first prizes in music festivals and had broadcast several times.   Many of the boys were also members of the three church choirs in the town, each run on professional lines.   S o o n after entering the school in 1938, Denis was given a voice test by Mr Smith and he immediately found himself in the choir. 'He then became my singing teacher and was really responsible for making me famous'.

'The choir practised every day and had to be present half-an-hour before the beginning of school, half an hour before afternoon school and sometimes after school as well.   All choir boys had a red satin material round the rear bottom edge of our caps, which made us stand out.   This was something to be proud of but some of the teachers hated us and didn't hesitate to show it with comments such as "come here, choir boy!" They never used our names.'

Very soon after Denis joined the school, the choir sang at the National Eisteddfod in Wales. 'It will be necessary to bring palliasses for your party,' the invitation ran.   'These can be made from ordinary hessian'. The boys left Mansfield at 7am on August 4th 1938 in the charge of Mr Smith and arrived in

Cardiff at 6pm. Arrangements had been made for them to stay at the Greenfield Open Air School, a building situated in beautiful surroundings about four miles from the city centre. Denis remembers that they had to fill their palliasses with straw obtained from a local farmer and make up their beds in an open-air shed!

On the following morning after rehearsing in a local secondary school they rode to The Pavilion where an audience of 14,000 awaited the competitors. Children's Day at the Eisteddfod opened with a violent storm but the clouds cleared before the 22 choirs assembled.

One of the test pieces was *My Land* by Olive Williams, a member of the adjudicating panel. Praising the High Oakham choir, she remarked that she had never until then heard the song rendered as she had intended. The boys were placed first and second in the two classes and won enough money to enable them to extend their stay until Saturday, touring the area and visiting the bays on the beautiful Gower Coast beyond Swansea. They left Cardiff on Sunday morning, arriving home to be greeted by a crowd of enthusiastic parents and friends.

The following year the choir, accompanied by Kathleen Holcombe, triumphed at the Mansfield Musical Festival which was adjudicated by the famous founder and conductor of the Glasgow Orpheus Choir. In his closing remarks, Sir Hugh Roberton was fulsome in his praise:

'This is a very exceptional body. There are not many choirs like this in the English-speaking world. Most artistic in temperament, they have everything - touch, tenderness, character and purity and naturalness of vowelling, and they cover a wide range of tone with never a blemish. The district holds no finer influence for good than the artistic work of these boys. This is the best junior choir in England - in <u>England</u>, mark you! These boys would no doubt be able to hold their own against any choir. It is genuine art, the whole thing so well governed, showing that quiet authority behind it all, which true art always has.'

Sir Hugh also complimented the boys on their use of the King's English. 'There is too much laxity in pronunciation these days,' he said, 'and if the King's English is good enough for a Scot, it should be for us!'

By this time, Harry Smith had approached Denis's mother with a view to teaching him to sing as a soloist. 'My mother told him that she could not afford to pay for lessons because she was already paying for piano tuition, so Harry Smith agreed to teach me for nothing, providing he could take half of everything I earned, plus expenses. He told my mother that I must stop my piano lessons and concentrate on singing. I have always regretted having to give up the piano, but I accepted the decision at the time.'

The first broadcast in which Denis participated with the school choir was in July 1939 from the new Nottingham Studio. The programme was transmitted live and Denis sang *Market Square* by Fraser Simpson and Schubert's *Cradle Song*. The broadcast opened with the choir singing *Orpheus with his Lute* by Edward German and concluded with *Lift Thine Eyes* from Mendelssohn's *Elijah*. Kathleen Holcombe was again accompanying the choir, Harry Smith playing for the solos.

Denis remembers the event as something of an ordeal. 'There we were, standing in the studio with the massive microphone hanging from the ceiling in the middle of the room. We took our places and sang our little hearts out. I had been told to practise the *Faery Song* by Rutland Boughton every morning for a week at school assembly to make sure I knew the piece well. When my turn came to broadcast, I stood confidently under the microphone. But at that moment Harry Smith called me to him and told me he had forgotten the music and I would have to sing *Market Square* instead. Can you imagine my panic? I nearly died. I asked Mr Smith if I could stand near him, so that I could look at the words on the piano, but he said "No! You will have to stand in the middle of the room under the microphone". Fortunately, I managed to get through it without faltering, but thinking about it now, I feel that Harry Smith had probably taught me the wrong song and did not want to admit it.'

A few weeks later, Denis came second in the solo and first with Robert Breedon in the duet sections of the Nottingham Musical Festival. Thereafter Denis came first in every music festival he entered and by the time he was fourteen he was asked if he would stop competing in order to give other boys a chance!

Although Denis had a great gift for singing, he acknowledges the debt he owes to Harry Smith. 'I would leave school at 4.15 pm and go to Mr Smith's home every day for tea. We would then start my singing lessons - scales, breathing, forming words to his satisfaction. I often didn't finish until 9 o'clock. After that he drove me home in his car and I went to bed. This was my regular routine, getting ready for concerts every weekend.'

During the first year of the war, Denis turned fourteen and left school to work in a local factory, though he continued to devote every spare minute to singing. During 1940, he sang at over one hundred concerts for the troops in the Mansfield area alone.

It was around this time that Denis became more widely known. In April 1941, Walter Legge at

HMV wrote to Harry Smith: 'If this soloist of yours is as good as your enthusiastic letter leads one to hope and expect, I shall be delighted to make a test record as you request. Would it be convenient for you to bring him on August 20th? Will you accompany him or shall I have Mr Gerald Moore here do that? Perhaps you will give me some indication of what you propose he should put on to wax?'

Denis remembers going to London by train on this and many other occasions. 'We always went on a Thursday on the *Aberdonian* from Nottingham and returned the following Tuesday. We stayed at the Regent Palace Hotel, which was very luxurious. Harry Smith had a 'sweet tooth' and, as sugar was scarce during the war, we had to be careful even though hotels were allowed extra rations. At breakfast -time Harry would tell me to hold the newspaper up so that he could put extra sugar in his tea without any- one else knowing. As he was also a very heavy smok- er, getting through as many as one hundred cigarettes a day, he would send me to buy extra supplies for him. Sometimes the shop assistant would not sell them to me as I was quite small and also still under age. However, when I was refused, Harry Smith was never anywhere to be seen!'

The first test recordings were made at HMV's Abbey Road Studios and in September Mr Smith received the news that these had been successful. In October Denis, accompanied by Gerald Moore, recorded five songs, of which two, *The Last Rose of Summer* and *Cradle Song* were selected for issue. Two months later a further five songs were recorded though unfortunately, due to wartime shortages, they were never released. A single copy of each of the eight pressings was given to Harry Smith but, sadly, only *Market Square* survived to be included on *The Better*

Land. This published record, HMV B9231, was issued in December 1941, selling at 3s.8d. It excited impressive reviews in the often critical *Gramophone* magazine:

'Hail to Master Denis Wright who, in my opinion, has made the best boy soprano record since the spacious days of Master Ernest Lough. The newcomer's voice has not the absolutely even drawn thread quality of Lough's. It is more of a <u>true</u> soprano, with the slightest tremolo, which is very attractive'.

In the November issue we read: 'He sings *The Last Rose of Summer* and Schubert's *Cradle Song* in one of the sweetest falsettos it is possible to imagine. You will find this a masterpiece of its type'. Denis was hailed as the successor to Ernest Lough. The *HMV Record Review* said: 'The voice is so exquisitely pure and has two attributes rarely found in boy sopranos - warmth and tenderness. Master Denis has been so musically taught that he phrases with a grace and sensitivity that many a woman might envy and emulate.'

In October 1941, Denis was invited to broadcast live from the Grand Theatre Llandudno with the famous Kentucky Minstrels, a group which comprised the BBC Variety & Male Voice Chorus with baritone soloist John Duncan. Also participating regularly in the twice monthly show were three black singing comedians, Ike Hatch, and Scott & Whaley. The choir was conducted by Leslie Woodgate, and the programme was compèred by Fred Yule and produced by Harry S. Pepper and Doris Arnold. Billy Ternent and his famous dance band were also featured. 'Fred Yule used to stand on the side of the stage with boards, telling the audience when to laugh!' Denis recalls.

Denis's first broadcast with the Kentucky Minstrels was a resounding success. 'After the broadcast we all ended the day with a fish and chip meal at Sumner's Café in Llandudno, and I remember the waitress bringing me the largest fish I had ever seen.'

The Mansfield papers reported that 'Denis Wright, who is fifteen-years-of-age, was a soloist in the Kentucky Minstrels Show broadcast in the Forces Programme on Monday. Mr Smith, who has been entirely responsible for his training, considers him the finest boy singer the school has had. He acquitted himself very well in the song *The Better Land* in which he was accompanied by the Minstrels' choir and the BBC Theatre Orchestra. Miss Doris Arnold, who invited Denis to broadcast and made a special arrangement of the song, will write music for other songs he will sing.'

Denis appeared with the Kentucky Minstrels regularly for nearly a year. In addition to *The Better Land*, Doris Arnold arranged for him Fraser-Simpson's setting of *Christopher Robin is Saying his Prayers* from *When we were very young* by A.A. Milne. He first broadcast this in the Forces Programme in February 1942 and later recorded both songs for HMV at the Kingsway Hall, London. Although Reginald Foort was the regular organist with The Kentucky Minstrels, Robinson Cleaver was at the organ for the recording, which was made in the same year.

In order to broadcast regularly, Denis became a member of C.E.M.A. (Council for the Encouragement of Music and the Arts). 'Although the payment for appearing in concerts was around three guineas, I was paid ten guineas a minute by the BBC for time on air. I would have to give Harry Smith half of that and also pay for both our expenses out of my share! I usually managed to take fifteen guineas home to my mother. She was very grateful to have this money but I do not think she had really considered the implications of her agreement with Mr Smith - he was way ahead of her in that respect.'

At the end of October 1941, a week after his first appearance with The Kentucky Minstrels, Denis went to the Colston Hall in Bristol to record a number of hymns with the local Greenbank Children's Choir. These were to be used in Uncle Mac's *Children's Hour* at a later date and HMV issued the records commercially. Sixty years after the recording, Denis and I went to Broadcasting House in Bristol, where he was interviewed for national television. As the result of an appeal, two members of the Greenbank Girls' Choir were traced and in a strange twist to the tale, Denis's brief appearance on television was seen by a long-lost niece in Scotland, who shouted to her husband, 'That's my uncle!' They had not met for over forty years and were delighted to be reunited.

In December 1941 Denis was again in Bangor to rehearse for the second of a series of six musical plays entitled *Behind the Laughter*, devised and written by Wee Georgie Wood. Described as a 'romance of the circus and the music halls', the plays featured the story of Syd Fletcher, the child of a circus family, who was born in 1898 and lived through the Music Hall Strike of 1907. In the second episode Charles Hawtrey, who played the young Syd, was to sing *Bonnie Mary of Argyll* on the stage of the Sun Music Hall and Denis was engaged to be the character's singing voice.

'I had to make my voice break during the song,' Denis recalls, 'and this was very upsetting for my mother who, hearing the live broadcast, thought it really had broken. She needed to be reassured it was just part of the play.'

However it wasn't just a life of broadcasting and recording: by the age of fourteen Denis was in full time employment with Royce's Shoe Company in

Mansfield.   The proprietor's daughter, Miss Evelyn Royce, took a special interest in his singing career and arranged for him to take as much time off as necessary.   On many occasions Denis would leave Mansfield on Thursday mornings and not return until the following Tuesday.   'As soon as I got back, I had to report to Miss Royce's office and give her a 'blow by blow' account of everything I had done over the weekend!   She was marvellous, and were it not for her kindness, I should not have been bringing a regular wage home to my mother - I was paid a weekly 10s/3d (51p) by Miss Royce, though this was nothing when compared to my professional fees.'

In March 1942 as a result of the success of previous broadcasts and Denis's two records, the High Oakham choir made a recording at the Leeds Station for a world broadcast to North and South America, Australia, South Africa and the Pacific.   The press announced that Denis Wright, 'the famous boy soprano, who has so long been associated with the choir', was the soloist.   Ronald Biggs, (the Director of Music, Northern Region) had a few weeks before visited the school and offered Mr Smith the engagement.   It was reported that the Local Education Authority had agreed to the invitation 'with great pleasure', a letter of thanks being sent to Mr Smith stating that not only had he improved the musical education of the children attending the school but he had done something which would be of [long] benefit to the town.   I managed to trace the announcer's script for the recording:

'This is London calling – Britain Sings - Today's programme in this series will be given by a choir of boys from High Oakham Central School with their conductor - Harry Smith.'   The opening two items, *The Road to the Isles*, and *All through the night*, in which Denis sang a solo, were followed by the com-

ment that 'such sensitive singing is all the more strik-
ing against its natural background. High Oakham
School is in the heart of the Nottinghamshire coal-
fields. It is a day school, the four hundred boys who
attend it coming from families actively engaged in
coal-mining or its attendant industries.' The programme went on to include *Vespers* by Fraser
Simpson, *Oft in the stilly night*, Brahms' *Cradle Song*
sung by Denis and *The Kerry Dance* by Molloy. It was
reported in the press that the present choir was a particularly young one, but 'it has fully maintained the
high traditions of its predecessors'.

No longer at school, Denis was able to fulfil a
large number of engagements. 'I was asked by the
composer Harry Farjeon if I would be willing to sing
in one of his works at a Promenade Concert at the
Royal Albert Hall on July 10th 1942, under the direction of Sir Henry Wood with the London
Philharmonic Orchestra. It was really a dream come
true.'

'We were told that the score for this composition, *Pannychis*, and the poem written by Eleanor
Farjeon, the composer's sister, would arrive in good
time for me to practise, but it had still not arrived
when the day of rehearsal came. We had to leave
Mansfield without the music, and we were already at
the railway station in Nottingham when a voice over
the tannoy announced that a package for Harry Smith
was at the Station Master's office awaiting collection.
Harry Smith's wife, Marjorie, contacted Councillor
Frank Hardy, a Gentleman's Tailor and Outfitter in
Nottingham Road, and he rushed it over to us in his
car. I had to study the score on the train journey but
at least it gave me some idea of what it was all about.
Learning music was not difficult for me at that age!'
Sometimes Denis's working relationship with Harry

Smith was not all that might be imagined. 'He was a very difficult teacher, and could be quite cruel.   On that day whilst I was trying to learn the music on the train he would employ his favourite trick of twisting my thumb each time I went wrong, which ensured I didn't make the same mistake again.

'The rehearsals for *Pannychis* took place at Harry Farjeon's flat, which contained three pianos, and there were sheets of music everywhere.   He was a small person with long unkempt hair, living almost as a rich hermit.   My stay in London was wonderful; I had meals at the Lyons Corner House, very often in the company of professionals like Alvar Liddell, the BBC announcer and baritone.   I also spent a few hours with the orchestra and Sir Henry Wood, practising my song.'

The Prom itself was a tremendous success and was well-documented in the press. One Mansfield newspaper report suitably captured both the atmosphere and excitement of the event:

'It is the interval in the Promenade Concert. The floor of the Albert hall is packed solid with people.   Consulting their programmes, the audience sees that the soloist is Denis Wright, the well-known Mansfield singer.   The interval ends.   The orchestral players come in, take their seats, tune up their instruments.   Sir Henry Wood smiles benignly.   The conductor, Basil Cameron, enters with Denis, who sits on the piano stool recently occupied by the pianist Solomon, who has just played Beethoven's *Emperor Concerto*. [There is] a murmur of surprise.   "Why, he's only a schoolboy!"

'The music [begins and] the fifth section is reached, the Song.   The boy, who has watched and listened, detaches himself from the piano stool, comes forward, and sings.   Some of the promenaders stand on tip-toe. The Albert Hall has witnessed many beautiful, exciting, amusing and moving incidents, but nothing more moving than this. [The boy has] a lovely voice, effortless, free, and has given to the rapt audience the charm of this new song.

'At the end there is a cry for the composer, who comes from his box by the platform. He turns to the singer, draws him to the front, and presents him to the audience. And how they respond! This is the loudest applause of the evening; for we know that his lovely voice will soon remain with us only through recordings and in our memories.'

Following the success of the Promenade Concert, Denis continued to be much in demand, both at HMV and singing for CEMA at venues in the East Midlands. Two weeks after the Prom he was back in London – at the Kingsway Hall - making his most enduring record, *The Better Land*. He was paid royalties on all his records, and on average three guineas for each concert performance, although, as we can confirm by the original contract, everything was sent directly to his manager, Harry Smith!

In September 1942, Denis received an invitation to take part in a two- and-a-half-hour version of *Julius Caesar* in which Marius Goring was to play Anthony, Valentine Dyall Brutus, and Eric Portman Cassius. Lucius's song was specially composed for Denis by John Ireland, the lute accompaniment played by Diana Poulton. The speaking part of Lucius was played by Roy Bradbury, a fellow member of the High Oakham choir. Denis and Roy stayed three nights in London with Harry Smith for which subsistence was paid at 17 shillings per night and the train fare from Mansfield to London was one pound nine shillings and a penny!

Denis adds: 'By this time I was sixteen-and-a-

half and I still had my voice but it was becoming lower, so I decided to join the forces, knowing full well that I was shortly due to be called up for National Service. I chose the RAF because, despite my singing commitments, I had found time to join the Air Training Corps in Mansfield.

'When Sir Hugh Roberton, the conductor of the Glasgow Orpheus Choir, heard about this he advised me not to sing, not to shout, not to smoke, and to give my voice a complete rest for a few years. This he maintained should stand me in good stead for its return later on.'

Denis was later posted to India and whilst there the pianist Solomon, who had been a fellow performer at the recent Prom, gave a recital for the troops in Delhi so the two men were able to renew their acquaintance.

Denis took Sir Hugh Roberton's advice and after he was demobbed in 1947 he went to see Harry Smith to ask what he thought of his 'new' voice. 'Harry told me the best thing to do would be to join the Mansfield Male Voice Choir (of which he was the conductor) and give my voice some training, so I began singing tenor, then second tenor, then baritone. I continued to sing in that choir for forty years as their principal soloist before deciding to join Bestwood Male Voice Choir near Nottingham, where I remained for ten years.

'Singing has been my life; I have had a wonderful time, both as a boy and as a baritone. God gave me this gift, and with the help of a good teacher, I was able to enjoy my singing and give pleasure to the listening public. I would never have changed a single moment.' After the war Denis spent his working life as a bus driver and Garage Clerk in Charge on the Mansfield and District Traction Company. He then worked as an ambulance driver for the disabled.

Denis Wright and his wife Margherita now live only a mile or two from Denis's childhood home. Like the other 'boys' featured on *The Better Land,* he has lived his adult life in the shadow of his childhood fame. For many years Denis's achievements lay forgotten and it is now fitting to celebrate again his career as a boy soprano, his recordings a testament to the achievements of the past. When Denis recorded his solo with the Kentucky Minstrels in 1942, no-one could have forecast that sixty years later his singing would delight another generation and bring memories back to those few remaining who remember the song and the better land of which he sang.

Denis Wright, Stephen Beet, and Major Denis Barthel, M.B.E. in 2000

Derek Barsham

Born in North London in 1930, Derek Barsham was an only child of musical parents. Before her marriage, his mother had been a singer and his father was a capable pianist. From an early age Derek had sung with local church choirs but in 1942 he joined the 1st Enfield Company of the Boys' Brigade, as a result of a chance meeting with Dr Leslie Ridge, a local GP and Captain ('Skipper') of the Company.

One Sunday in Bible Class, during the singing of the Brigade hymn *Father who hast made us brothers* Derek's voice could be heard above the others, and Dr Ridge, who had long wished to discover a boy soprano of the calibre of Ernest Lough, asked if he could take him to see Percy Jackson, a well-known local singing teacher. Jackson remarked that all he needed to do was to improve Derek's breathing as he felt the boy had a pure and natural voice of excellent quality.

So it was that Derek began his musical training and in September 1943 Dr Ridge, now acting as his manager, wrote to May Jenkin, ('Aunty Elizabeth') the Assistant Director of BBC Children's Hour asking if she would hear him – and assuring her that he was 'of charming presence' ! Derek was invited to come on November 18th bringing with him 'ten minutes of suitable material.' He remembered the occasion vividly and recalled being shown the newsroom which was guarded by a sentry armed with a rifle and fixed bayonet!

The following day Miss Jenkin wrote that Derek 'not only has a charming voice but has been beautifully trained and his pianissimo singing is particularly lovely.' It was hoped that they might fit him into a programme to go out early on Christmas morning and two weeks later confirmation came that Derek McCulloch ('Uncle Mac') required him to pre-record three carols accompanied by Percy Jackson at the piano.

As a result of his Christmas broadcast Derek immediately became well-known, though this led to some unwelcome attention from certain of his contemporaries at Chase Side School in Enfield. 'I would walk across the play-ground and someone would shout "There's that sissy singer," and I would be set upon and given a good bashing by a group of boys. At the end of the school day I would try to wait until they had left but they were always at the gate to trap me. So I decided to climb over the back wall and run along the railway embankment which took me close to where I lived. One day I found them waiting for me there so I ran the gauntlet and leapt through the hedge (partially demolishing it in the process) to the safety of my back garden. As soon as I entered the house a brick flew through the window. My mother called the police and the headmaster was informed.'

The Enfield Schoolboy

The bullying eventually died down however – and Derek's prowess on the football field certainly helped. Many years later he gave a concert at Pentonville Gaol and recognised one of his former tormentors in the audience!

Dr Ridge was a high principled man who from the outset was concerned that Derek's talent should not be 'commercialised' or exploited in any way. He was determined that Derek should sing to the glory of God and in honour of the Boys' Brigade. But his unwillingness for Derek to accept any fees for his singing soon caused difficulty in his dealings with the BBC. Early in 1944 Derek was asked by Arthur Wynn at the Music Department to come for an audition (this time with a professional accompanist) and it was decided that some studio recordings should be made for use on air when required. However Uncle Mac stipulated that 'we could not contemplate asking Derek to make these

Derek Barsham, winner of the Talent Pascal Cup, Enfield, 1943

recordings without suitable remuneration,' a condition which Dr Ridge appears to have accepted.

In wartime the BBC Children's Hour programme was followed by the chimes of Big Ben and the famous "V" signals before the 6 o'clock news bulletin. On a couple of occasions Derek sang at the very end of the programme and it was sobering to be told by Uncle Mac that perhaps a hundred million listeners had by that time tuned in.

In 1944 Derek left school and enrolled as a student at Enfield Technical College – though his attendance there must have been at best sporadic! By this time there were more and more opportunities to perform in live concerts and he sang on his fourteenth birthday at the Swan Electric Company in Enfield, the local Gazette reporting that 'his lovely clear voice rang out across the canteen.' After his performance he was shown round the Apprentices' Training Department having expressed an interest in engineering.

There were also concerts further afield in the home counties and far beyond. The press reviews of these were invariably enthusiastic and one reporter noticed that he had 'a mischievous twinkle in his eye and a very good appetite.'

In May 1944 Derek was involved in the first of four annual Boys' Brigade rallies at the Royal Albert Hall in London. *The Daily Telegraph* noted that nearly 3,000 members took part. A silver band played and there was a torch-lit tattoo and displays of drill, gymnastics, first-aid and signalling. 'Private Derek Barsham' brought the event to a conclusion 'by singing an evening hymn in a beautiful soprano voice.'

Lessons with Percy Jackson continued, though on one occasion Derek's cycle ride to his teacher's home proved to be a terrifying experience. He had set off but then realised he had left some of the music at home. He turned back halfway to fetch it and when he set out again he heard a huge explosion and saw a tower of smoke rising into the air ahead of him. Almost immediately ambulances and fire engines were flying past. Had he not forgotten to bring a couple of songs he would have been at the very spot a V2 rocket landed!

Dr. Leslie Ridge

Derek's repertoire at

this time consisted of folksongs, classical songs, patriotic songs, an occasional sentimental ballad, and sacred songs or arias by composers ranging from Handel to Howells. Some of them would, these days, be considered unsuitable for a young boy! Dr Ridge had long hoped that a recording-company would take an interest in his protégé and (after a disappointing response from HMV who had achieved enormous sales with Ernest Lough's discs made in the late 1920s) he seems to have been successful in negotiations with Decca, though no correspondence about these has survived.

Early on in 1945 Decca released Derek's recording of Stephen Adams' *The Star of Bethlehem* and *The Holy City* accompanied by the young American organist, Fela Sowande. The recording session for this had lasted all day on account of frequent interruptions because of enemy aircraft flying overhead. The disc received a cautious review from Alec Robertson in *Gramophone* magazine of April 1945: 'Derek Barsham is not another Master Lough … nevertheless this is a good voice.' Christopher Stone in *Record Review* was more enthusiastic. 'You have here … a real big winner. The absence of … emotional vibrato … is - well it's a revelation. And, so far as one may judge … his voice still has a long run.'

But now further difficulties were arising at the BBC owing to Dr Ridge's moral scruples and his feelings of responsibility towards Derek. He had turned down many invitations for him to perform, and when it was discovered that excerpts from a BBC recording of Derek singing *O for the wings of a dove* had been played no fewer than nine times during a light-hearted play broadcast in early April 1945 he was horrified.

To Arthur Wynn he wrote: 'I was really distressed that Derek's name, coupled as it is in the pub-

lic ear with the name of the Boys' Brigade was mentioned in association with a farcical comedy [*Fly away
Herbert* by Gordon Glover] which eulogises the drink-
ing habit. I hope that you will cut out his name from
any future transmission of this play'. Later on, he was
to object to Derek's participation in the programme
Variety Bandbox. Charity concerts met with Dr Ridge's
approval, however, and many and varied were the
good causes for which Derek sang. Notable among
these was the Spitfire Mitchell Memorial Fund for
which an evening of entertainment was organised in
the Guildhall, Southampton in March 1946.

Sharing the bill with Derek on that occasion
were Richard Murdoch and Tommy Handley.
According to the *Southampton Evening News* 'Derek
Barsham … deservedly won as much applause as
anyone in the show. Complete recordings will enable
future generations to enjoy his unusually limpid and
resonant singing.'

It was as early as January 1945 that Dr Ridge
had the idea that it would be suitable for Derek to
receive a Royal Command. Accordingly, he wrote to
Sir Alan Lascelles asking if Their Majesties would like
Derek to sing in the presence of the Princesses, a
request turned down because of 'so many claims
being made on their Royal Highnesses' time.' Not to
be deterred, Dr Ridge wrote again in March asking if
the Princesses would accept an advance copy of
Derek's new record (of *The Holy City*) and also advis-
ing of the day and time of his next broadcast.

Derek was out at a football practice on VE Day
in May 1945. A whole year earlier he had recorded
Elgar's *Land of Hope and Glory* for the BBC in antici-
pation of the victorious day. Now, as he returned
home on his bicycle he heard his own voice emanat-
ing from wireless sets along his road and realised that

- yes – the war had ended!

June 1945 saw another Boys' Brigade rally in the Royal Albert Hall, and this year the theme was "East meets West". In the (often politically incorrect!) words of the *Brigade Gazette*: 'the [imaginary] year was 1965 and the scene darkest Africa. We delighted in the crowd of jolly "black" Boys who so obviously delighted in their change of complexion – especially when afterwards proceeding unwashed to tea in Kensington. We heard the "invaders" arriving by air – the sudden cutting off of the engine sending a nasty reminiscent shiver down our spines [because of the wartime doodle bugs]. The "natives", rightly in our view, resented the aggression, and when the "white men," complete with burdens, marched in, a tense situation developed. But by good fortune the West Kent [Boys' Brigade] company had kidnapped Enfield's BBC nightingale and his unsurpassable rendering of a missionary hymn … improved "international relations".'

Dr Ridge's anxiety that Derek's voice would not last much longer now prompted him to urge the BBC for more engagements 'in the hope that [the listening public] could have the pleasure of hearing him before that tragic day when his voice breaks.' In one reply Douglas Lawrence, Acting Light Music Supervisor, replied that he had 'by no means forgotten him' but that 'after each occasion I am simply inundated with letters from choirmasters etc who say they have boys who can sing equally well and even better … Putting a boy soprano on the air can be a very thankless task.'

Nevertheless Dr Ridge persisted in his requests for further broadcasting opportunities, assuring the BBC that Derek's voice ' is holding out almost miraculously' and thanking them sincerely for their help and encouragement in previous years. More engagements were indeed forthcoming in 1946 and Decca released further discs in that year and the next, though not always in the chronological order of their being recorded. For instance, a disc of Mendelssohn's *Hear my prayer* & *O for the wings of a dove* accompanied by the High Wycombe Male Voice Choir conducted by Leslie Woodgate (Decca's first Full Frequency Range vocal recording) had been made early in 1945 but was not on sale until a year later. There were two more songs accompanied by Fela Sowande, two accompanied by the Phil Green String Sextet and, eventually, four songs accompanied by the pianist Phyllis Spurr. These and all of Derek's recordings are available on *The Better Land* series.

1st Enfield Compnay, The Boys Brigade, 1946

The 1946 Boys' Brigade rally in London was not (according to the *Enfield Gazette*) easy to describe. Billed as a "Physical Phantasmagoria", there was a 'central, a prefabricated, chromium plated self-illuminated telephone kiosk de luxe. At the end … through the roof of this silver palace emerged Lance- Corporal Derek Barsham who … sang [Eric Coates' *The Star of God*] wonderfully, with moving effect' (see photograph!). The occasion was filmed and Derek's singing (accompanied, unfortunately, by some inexpert piano playing) was on the soundtrack.

In June of 1946 Derek was scheduled to appear as soloist in a festival of choirboys at Westminster Abbey, but, just a few days before the event, he was taken seriously ill with peritonitis following a burst appendix and had to spend three weeks in hospital. Dr Ridge's help at this time was invaluable and was in no small part responsible for the rapid recovery which followed. All July and August engagements were cancelled but by September Derek was apparently back to normal. Local concert engagements resumed and in early October he sang (in aid of Barnardo's) with the London Symphony Orchestra at the Central Hall Westminster. There were further broadcasts and a visit to Oxford to give a recital in the chapel of Balliol College, the proceeds of which were sent to the Enfield hospital where he had recently been a patient.

In November the local *Gazette* reported: 'Derek is now sixteen but Dame Nature for once is extending her favours and his voice is as beautiful (if not more so) than ever.' By this time Derek had left the Technical College and had started working in a bank. But hardly had he begun there than he had to take five weeks' unpaid leave to attend rehearsals for a concert performance of Musorgsky's opera *Boris Godunov* in which he sang the part of Fyodor, son of Boris (sung

by Norman Lumsden). The orchestra was the London Symphony Orchestra and the conductor Stanford Robinson. The opera was broadcast live in the Home Service on February 12th 1947, and two days later a BBC recording was made for later transmission on the new Third Programme. Two short excerpts were also recorded by Decca, and a few days later Derek's final record – on

Derek Barsham's last broadcast as a boy soprano, a few weeks before his 17th birthday

which he sang two Brigade hymns – was made. Fittingly it was one of those hymns which had first caught the attention of Dr Ridge in the Bible Class five years earlier.

Just before making this final disc in May, Derek had sung for one last time at the annual Boys' Brigade rally in the Royal Albert Hall. This time the event was relayed to other stations via the BBC overseas network, as well as to the USA. Afterwards a surprise awaited - a chance to fulfil one of Derek's (and his mother's!) ambitions. Commentator John Ellison was there to interview him for the popular Saturday evening radio programme *In Town Tonight*. In the 1940s this was fame indeed!

Derek was now advised to rest his voice for two years in the hope that it would retain its qualities in a lower register. Dr Ridge's final correspondence with Buckingham Palace was to ask, on behalf of the Boys' Brigade, if H.R.H. Princess Elizabeth would accept a copy of Alan Murray's *I'll walk beside you* (a disc released earlier in 1947) 'as a token of our loyalty and respectful congratulations … on the occasion of her forthcoming marriage from Derek Barsham and myself.'

Derek's career as a boy soprano had ended, though, in a letter to the BBC Dr Ridge maintained that his voice 'never actually broke, but … is evolving into a rich baritone.' Derek had taken various jobs before eventually choosing to become a full time entertainer.

Derek Barsham's first public performance, after his boyhood career ended, was with the Band of the Irish Guards at Alexandra Palace, 1951.

Having resumed his singing career in 1952 he decided that he needed a new stage name. 'No-one could spell "Barsham" so I had to think of an alternative. Then I remembered that when I left Chase School my headmaster wrote in my autograph book "Always be a man," so that's what I became.'

For over twenty-five years Derek Mann was a Cruise Director for several companies including the Royal Viking Line where he met his wife, Barbara. He is, in 2005, still a full-time singer and entertainer and lives in Cape Cod, USA.

The Martin Boys' Choir

Arthur Martin and Billy Neely

The Province of Ulster has produced several notable boy sopranos, of whom many were members of the once-famous Martin Boys' Choir. Born in Belfast in 1935, William Callin was brought up by the Neely family, taking their name and was thereafter known as Billy Neely. As a small child he developed a stutter, and it was decided that he should take up singing to help his speech difficulties. He was placed under the tutelage of Miss Nan Shaw, a respected Belfast singing teacher and it was soon discovered that not only had he a fine singing voice but that his stutter had completely disappeared. At around the same time, Billy joined the choir of his small Bangor primary school, where he was picked out as the boy with the most promising voice.

In 1946 Billy auditioned and was accepted for the choir of St. Anne's Cathedral, Belfast and he came under the influence of the formidable but much-respected choirmaster, Captain C.J. Brennan O.B.E., who had been in charge of the music at the cathedral since 1904 and went on to complete sixty years as organist.

'The singing in the choir in those days was quite superb,' Billy remarked 'and I cannot remember an unkind word being said, although everyone, including dear, kind Dean Elliott, was in complete awe of 'C.J.', as Captain Brennan was known. His word was absolute law. I admired him greatly and he was a very fine musician and teacher.'

Several members of the choir were also in Arthur Martin's Boys' Choir, formed a few years previously and which was making a name for itself far beyond Northern Ireland. Billy joined Martin's choir around 1948. He was then nearly 13 and had become one of the cathedral choir's leading soloists. He had, also through the help of Arthur Martin and Havelock

Nelson (Accompanist at the B.B.C.), already taken small parts in Children's Hour broadcasts in the Northern Ireland Home Service. Later that year he was the first Ulster boy to enter the prestigious Blackpool Music Festival, winning the Broadhead Trophy which was the first prize for boy sopranos by beating 66 other boys. The adjudicator, Miss Helen Henschel (the daughter of the composer, conductor and singer Sir George Henschel) said she had never heard such a beautiful voice. Shortly afterwards Billy travelled to Glasgow where, according to all accounts, 'he carried all before him!'

His first major B.B.C. recording was in September 1948 when he appeared in the pantomime *Jack and the Drainpipe*, broadcast from the Belfast Station in December.

'In those days the entire B.B.C. seemed to revolve around Children's Hour,' Billy said. 'Cicely Matthews, Head of Children's Hour, was a busy, bustling lady and both she and Havelock Nelson seemed to run everything. There was none of the sophisticated equipment we have today, just a single microphone in the studio. Everything went out live and the place was a hive of activity, almost a thoroughfare! Often people would walk in and out of the studio during my broadcasts, which could be quite unnerving!'

Havelock Nelson, the official B.B.C. accompanist, took a personal interest in Billy's career and became a good friend. He introduced him to the respected Ulster tenor, James Johnston, who sponsored Billy to appear in several concerts early in 1949. These concerts and early broadcasts were really the beginning of his professional career and his fame soon spread far beyond the Six Counties of Northern Ireland. He even presented his own variety programme and also appeared on the Irish Republic's Radio Eireann.

In March 1949 Billy again came first at the Blackpool Festival, and in May he won the boys' solo class at Glasgow. In second place came Master Robert Waddell, a member of the Kirkintilloch Junior choir. The press reported that 'the two boys congratulated each other, picked up their coats and cases and hurried to catch the night boat to Belfast', where they both took part in services at the Shankill Road Mission (also known as The Albert Hall) the following day.

The concerts sponsored by James Johnston had taken Billy all over the Province and in December he was topping the bill of what were described as 'B.B.C. Stars' at a recorded concert at the Ritz Cinema, Belfast. Billy and the baritone Norman Hawkins were accompanied by the Ulster Singers with Joseph Seal at the organ.

It was around this time that Billy agreed to leave St. Anne's Cathedral Choir in order to devote himself entirely to his singing career. 'C.J. was very kind about it but we decided that what I was doing was not compatible with the life and demands of a cathedral chorister. I missed the choir enormously and whenever I visited, Captain Brennan always greeted me most warmly and was greatly interested in my musical activities.'

Billy rounded off the year as soprano soloist in *Messiah* and in 1950 began with a series of engagements in London, arranged by James Johnston and Arthur Martin. He gave several concerts en route, notably in Manchester; and in London. James Johnston, who was contracted to H.M.V., arranged for a test recording session at Abbey Road Studios where Billy was introduced to the accompanist Gerald Moore. 'He was a kind-hearted and amusing man and had the most enormous hands – almost like a pugilist's. It never ceased to amaze me how such a wonderful pianist could have such stubby hands. He would often play little tricks on me during rehearsal, like suddenly playing the wrong tune to the song I was singing! I became very fond of him and he introduced me to Victoria de los Angeles and that wonderful mezzo-soprano Elena Gerhardt, who taught me so much about *Lieder*.' In fact both these ladies reported that they considered Billy's talent 'outstanding'.

It was during this first session at Abbey Road that Billy recorded Arensky's *Six Children's Songs*, which were released in October of that year. Victor Carne, the contracts manager, was anxious that more recordings were made before June when Billy would be 15 and 'at a dangerous age' as far as his voice was concerned! Subsequently, in June and October, two more recording sessions were arranged and five more discs were cut. Gerald Moore later obtained tapes of the masters which have survived to this day and are featured on the *Better Land* CD's.

Back home Billy was in even greater demand, making more broadcasts both from Broadcasting House in Belfast and for Radio Eireann, appearing with Arthur Martin, who sang baritone.

In March he was back in London with Johnston, who was 'determined to do something with

Billy Neely and acompanist, Samuel Barron

that voice of his'. Introducing the 14-year-old boy to the cast at Covent Garden, he said: 'Some day, perhaps, you will be greeting my successor: here he is!' Billy had a few days earlier been awarded first place in the Senior *Lieder* Class of the Belfast Music Festival competing against adult sopranos. Indeed he was the first boy to enter this prestigious competition. His accompanist, the young Samuel Barron, was a Queen's University student.

To be featured on the radio programme 'Henry Hall's Guest Night', was something of a privilege in those days, and Billy made three appearances, presenting items as varied as Ave *Maria* and *Smilin'*

Through. He had left Bangor Grammar School so that he could spend more time on his musical activities. In June he played Don Ettore in Haydn's opera *La Canterina* (*The Songsters*) produced by Havelock Nelson. Reviews of his appearance as the love-sick boy were impressive. Later that month he was back in London at the B.B.C. and recording for H.M.V.

Returning to Belfast he was in cabaret at the Midlands Ideal Homes Exhibition, billed as 'Belfast's Own Boy Soprano' and throughout September he took a major part in a C.E.M.A. (Council for the Encouragement of Music and the Arts) tour of Northern Ireland, beginning at the Protestant Hall, Ballymena and finishing in Londonderry. Appearing with Billy was the celebrated young cellist Florence Hooton, and the pianist Maurice Cole.

'It is quite impossible to distinguish between the merits of the three,' 'Rathcol' of *The Belfast Telegraph* noted. 'When Billy appeared on stage [in Ballymena] there was a resounding burst of applause, and when he began to sing, there was not a movement in the hall. This talented lad, who has conquered hearts all over the United Kingdom with his beautiful voice, made yet another conquest ... The boy sings with all the assurance of a prima donna of 25 years' experience. Happily, he is just a lively lovable lad of fifteen, whose only wish after the concert was to play tennis with one of the boys. Asked if his voice was tired, he replied: "No, I only sang twelve songs" – and, I may add, two encores.'

Throughout this three-week tour with his friend Havelock Nelson as his accompanist, Billy's voice, described as 'almost at maturity', was praised by every critic. Arrangements did not always go according to plan, however, and the closing concert in the Guildhall, Londonderry, was far from uneventful.

'Music has that great value of having no political or religious barriers,' opined the *The Belfast Telegraph*, 'although one "lady" did not think so and believed that the occasion was opportune to stage a "demonstration" of her own. In her childlike simplicity, while Mr. Cole was playing the National Anthem, she thought it was the right moment to walk down the aisle, continuing between the audience and the stage, and out.'

Reminding us of the strict sectarian divisions of those days, the reporter went on to explain that the pianist had given full warning of his intent to play the Anthem following his encore, 'yet this lady remained for it and directly insulted the artiste, whom she must have known came from across the Channel.' *The Telegraph* suggested that it might be better in future if the National Anthem were played at the beginning of a concert – 'so that anyone who cannot wait a few minutes will leave – and perhaps NOT come back'.

At the end of this highly successful C.E.M.A. tour, Billy broadcast Mendelssohn's *Hear my prayer* from London and appeared at the Central Hall, Westminster with Belfast's Ormiston Choir. Around this time Arthur Martin decided it was time for Billy to rest his voice. The script of Billy's final broadcast on Christmas Eve in the prestigious programme 'Grand Hotel' survives. He also, like Derek Barsham before him, had the honour of being interviewed on the popular Saturday talk show 'In Town Tonight'. It was all a fitting end to Billy's teenage singing career as a boy soprano. He was just over fifteen years of age.

Billy's records sold well and were frequently broadcast for many years. In 1950 he had been described as 'Northern Ireland's highest paid boy soprano'. In *The Gramophone*, Moore Orr regarded the recordings of Durante's *Vergin tutt' amor and*

Marcello's *Il mio bel foco* as 'the finest example of the work of a boy soprano that the gramophone has yet given us', and reviewing *The Coventry Carol* in 1952, the celebrated broadcaster Richard Dimbleby wrote: 'His was one of the loveliest treble voices I have heard.'

Billy Neely, with the constant support and help of his friend and mentor, Arthur Martin realized his ambition and won a three-year scholarship – the Seguin Award – to the Royal Academy of Music in 1954. He studied theory, harmony, composition and piano. Four years later, as Lawrence Neely, he won the William Robertshaw Exhibition. Under his professional name, Billy distinguished himself as a baritone and appeared in many rôles throughout the 1950s.

Billy met his future wife, Jenny, at the Royal Academy. They married in 1960 making their life in France, where they have lived ever since. Arthur Martin had been a great influence on Billy and had given the boy a great love of fine art and it was this interest that was to provide him with a future career. In 2004 , William Corkill-Callin and his family continue a successful business in antiques and textiles, travelling all over France and the United Kingdom.

I was able to trace Billy Neely through the good offices of William Adair, an accompanist of Arthur Martin's Boys' Choir and Dr. Harry Grindle, formerly choirmaster at St. Anne's Cathedral. Neither Billy nor his wife had listened to any of his records in forty years. 'We were both deeply moved when we sat down and played them together after your contacting us in 1999' Billy said. 'So many memories came flooding back and I realized, perhaps for the first time since I was a boy, just how much it all meant to me at the time. I wish I could re-live the whole experience!'

Billy Neely and Stephen Beet
at Wesley's Chapel, May 2000

It was during the time that Billy Neely was singing that Arthur Martin realized his ambition of forming a boys' concert choir in Belfast. He seemed to be not impressed with the popular 'angelic head-tone' cultivated by choirmasters in those days, and instead conceived the idea of training boys to sing in concert and on the stage. Martin cultivated a clean fresh vocal tone in his boys and he also sought new repertoire in addition to the rather sentimental music so beloved of the pre-war public. Perhaps for this reason, and due to the excellence of the choir's soloists, the composer Benjamin Britten was moved to write music especially for Martin's boys and to select several of the choir's soloists for his operas. The choir was not affiliated to any church or organization, although Martin was organist of the Shankill Road Mission, known as 'The Albert Hall'. Rehearsals took place once a week in a hired room, adjacent to a cafe in College Square, Belfast.

Although Martin was not against his boys singing the popular sentimental songs so beloved of the public, his accompanist William Adair recalls his selecting the best classical and folk music sometimes of an unusual nature. 'He was always on the lookout for something new,' he remarked., 'and he from time to time discovered real gems such as Merikanto's little -known *A Fairy story by the fire,* realized so movingly-by Billy Neely.'

Desmond Morrow came to prominence short-ly after Billy Neely had finished singing and was much featured throughout the 1951-4 season of con-certs, often in the part of Bastien in *Bastien and Bastienne* (Mozart's opera, written at the age of 12). Another popular operetta of the day was *The New Master* or *Cupid in the Classroom...An Operetta for Boys in one act* by Heathcote Statham. In fact Morrow, who was 13 in 1952, was principal soloist during this peri-od, singing much of the repertoire previously selected for Billy. Sadly, Desmond, who was the son of Billy Morrow, a correspondent on *The Belfast Telegraph*, was tragically killed in a motor accident in his early 30s.

Early in 1954 Ronnie Preston became the third of Martin's boys to win the Broadhead Trophy at the Blackpool Festival. *The Belfast Telegraph* congratulat-ed Arthur Martin, reporting that 'Belfast has the secret of superb boy soprano singing: great boys and a great teacher!' The fine reputation of the choir's soloists was enhanced when Michael Hartnett came to promi-nence. Hartnett was one of the few Catholic boys in the choir and remembers his trepidation at the prospect of venturing into 'foreign territory' in order to attend practices and concerts, which were generally held in Protestant halls and places of worship. The carol services and concerts of 1955 gave Michael his first opportunity of success. Early the following year, he won the Milling Cup at the Carrickfergus Music Festival, having been awarded the highest marks ever in the festival. Kenneth Montgomery of Belfast, also a member of the choir, came second. The adjudicator took the unusual step of inviting Michael to repeat his performance at the evening session in order that the adult competitors could hear his singing.

Meanwhile, 13-year-old Ronnie Preston, already a veteran of seven broadcasts, was again on the air both at the B.B.C. and at Radio Eireann, where

Benjamin Britten, Michael Hartnett and Arthur Martin

he presented a programme of early Italian songs. In 1956, Benjamin Britten was introduced to Arthur Martin by an agent, Colin Graham, and Britten agreed to audition Michael Hartnett to understudy the part of 'Miles' in his opera *The Turn of the Screw*, which was to be staged at the Scala Theatre, London. David Hemmings, who played Miles, was nearly 15 and his understudy, Robin Fairhurst (Head Boy of The Temple Church, London), was nearly a year older. It was therefore obvious that another Miles would have to be found and Michael, being so much younger, was the obvious candidate.

After his visit to Aldeburgh, Michael travelled to London for rehearsals during October. There he received some tuition from Lawrence Neely, who was

studying at the Royal Academy of Music. Appearing with Hemmings in the opera were Peter Pears and Joan Cross. During the performance, Michael was given just one opportunity of playing the part of Miles – on 25th October - co-starring with Peter Pears. He had just turned 13 and acquitted himself with real distinction. Arthur Martin, who was with Michael in London, introduced another soloist, Sean Haldane, to Britten, who agreed to feature the boy the following season. Britten was so impressed with Hartnett's interpretation of the rôle of Miles that he decided the boy would be Hemmings' successor. He was invited to appear in Paris as Hemming's understudy and to tour Canada with Britten's New English Opera Group. It was during the Paris performance that Hemming's voice finally broke in mid performance, when he was replaced by Fairhurst. Directly after the London performance both Sean and Michael returned to Belfast where they appeared in several concerts over the Christmas season.

Sean Haldane was a member of St. Peter's Church, Belfast, and had come to the notice of Arthur Martin after the boy returned from a Royal School of Church Music course at Exeter Cathedral earlier in 1956. As a member of Martin's choir, he was offered a part in Britten's *Let's Make an Opera* at Christmas. Sean was studying Irish, a passion he inherited from his father; around this time he won first prize at the Belfast Irish 'Feis'.

'An outrageous thing for a Protestant to do!' Sean said. 'Although Arthur Martin aimed to produce a boy's voice for use in opera, I had very much a traditional choirboy's head tone, which Arthur also liked, and he found music that was suited to my voice. He was a superb teacher and many boys owe a great deal to him. He was not a professional musician in the strict sense and had a good position on the railways,' Sean added.

In November another of the choir's soloists Raymond Quinn of Banbridge made his broadcast debut, singing *The crow, The* cuckoo, and *The first mercy* by Peter Warlock amongst other items. Reports of his 'delightful voice' appeared in the press.

The Northern Ireland tenor, James Johnstone, who had often sung with Billy Neely, appeared with Sean and Michael at the Broadway Cinema in the Falls Road in March 1957. The boys, now 14 and 13 respectively, were described as 'Martin's most experienced singers' and performed a selection of mainly classical and traditional folk music. Sean had made rapid progress as a soloist and his voice was described by the composer Michael Head as 'a thing of ethereal beauty'. No fewer than eight soloists appeared in a concert at Bloomfield, which comprised a varied selection of music ranging from Purcell's *Sound the trumpet* (with Sean and Michael) to contemporary items by Bantock and Finzi.

The 10th Aldeburgh Festival in 1957 marked the bicentenary of the death of Domenico Scarlatti,

Sean Haldane, George Malcolm, and Michael Hartnett

and at the gala performance of Britten's *Albert Herring* in the Jubilee Hall, Michael sang the part of Harry, appearing with Peter Pears, Joan Cross and Gladys Parr. The following Tuesday, both boys were accompanied by George Malcolm at the harpsichord in a programme of Italian music, marking the bicentenary of Domenico Scarlatti. Sean particularly remembers from that programme two motets, *Iste confessor* and

Salve Regina by Montiverdi. Arthur Martin described the boys' appearance at Aldeburgh as 'their greatest honour yet'. Afterwards the boys were presented to H.R.H. Princess Mary, the Princess Royal, and engaged in friendly conversation with Princess Margaret of Hess, a cousin of Prince Philip. Described for the first time by the press as 'boy trebles', both were praised for 'their angelic purity of voice.'

Directly after the festival, Michael returned to London to begin rehearsals for *The Turn of the Screw*, to be performed in Canada and the United States in August. The libretto, by Myfawny Piper, had been adapted from the novel by Henry James. The tour began with seven performances at the Stratford Shakespeare Festival at the Stratford Theatre, Ontario. *The Toronto Telegraph* wrote of the premier: '...a brilliant piece of theatre that moves steadily and with mounting climax to the death of Miles, played and sung so well by 13-year-old Michael Hartnett … We could find little fault with Master Hartnett except that projection was not always of top quality.'

The Daily Star was equally enthusiastic and printed a picture of Michael and his Canadian understudy, Billy Potton, who, it was claimed, was teaching Michael the rudiments of baseball. Michael's first performance in Stratford with Peter Pears was just his second appearance as the young Miles. Following severe criticism of the opening night stage arrangements, adjustments were made allowing for better projection. However, on one occasion Michael fell over on stage, nearly knocking himself out as he flung himself onto the bed, which was part of the set. 'I was dazed but managed to carry on and the audience just thought it was part of the scene.' *The New York Times* recommended *The Turn of the Screw* 'as an experience in contemporary music,' adding that 'critics unanimously accorded accolades to young Mike Hartnett, who has a superb voice coupled with dramatic ability.' Reactions to the rest of the cast were mixed and some, used to more 'melodious' works, did not appreciate the closely interwoven words and music that gave the opera its moments of beauty and horror.

Throughout the eight-week tour Michael was greeted with acclaim by the Canadian public. On one occasion he was even persuaded to give an impromptu rendition of *Danny Boy*. 'People were weeping all over the place,' he said.

The cast returned to Belfast via Germany, where Michael was taken behind the 'Iron Curtain', and was horrified to see a man severely beaten by thugs and left for dead in a street.

Back in Belfast Michael 'took the flu', as Arthur Martin described it. 'I thought his voice would recover but now it has broken.' Sean Haldane, a year his senior, took over all of Michael's engagements, including appearing with James Johnstone in *Messiah* that Christmas.

Earlier that year, Sean and three other boys, including Michael Crawford, had taken part in a recording of Britten's *A Boy was Born*, and Hartnett was the soloist in *Rejoice in the Lamb*, with the Purcell Singers, conducted by Imogen Holst (although Brtten is credited as conductor). The L.P. was issued by Decca in 1958. Unlike earlier records, this disc was made from taped masters, microgroove recording having replaced hot wax a few years previously. 'The performance can hardly be bettered.

'The soloists', said *The Record Review*, 'are uniformly perfect, especially Michael Hartnett, who is remarkably steady and true but retains just enough of that uncertainty which makes every far reaching excursion of a boy's voice a delicious adventure.'

Michael completed his studies in Belfast. He is now President of the Tillyard Management Corporation in Toronto, where he has lived with his wife Susan and their family for many years. A few years ago, Michael was driving home from Toronto when he heard his boyhood voice on the wireless. 'I called in and was put on the show but I don't think the presenter believed I was telling the truth when I told them I had been the boy they had just featured!'

Sean Haldane continued singing as a boy soprano until 1958 when he was fifteen. 'I was more

than ready to grow up by that time and my last performance as a boy soprano was *Hear my prayer*, which I sang with the Grimsby Choral Society. During my solo I found that I could not produce the first of several top g's: the notes just weren't there. When the lady conductor realized what was happening, she kindly supplied the note for me. After that I decided I would sing as a boy soprano no more.'

Sean Haldane in 1958

Sean was, however, a talented flautist and played with the Belfast Youth Orchestra for several years. He is now a Consultant Neuro Psychologist with the National Health Service and the author of several books of poetry and literary criticism.

Several of Arthur Martin's singers have become professional musicians. Kenneth Montgomery began his adult singing career at the Glyndebourne Festival Opera and the Sadler's Wells Opera. He was artistic and musical director of Opera Northern Ireland. Montgomery is also a regular guest conductor with orchestras throughout the world. Many of his recordings have been issued on LP and CD.

One of the last soloists to be trained by Arthur Martin was Kevin Platts, the original 'Cobweb' in Britten's *A Midsummer Night's Dream* at the 1960 Aldeburgh Festival. He also sang the rôle of 'Spirit' in Britten's edition *of Dido and Aeneas* staged at Drottningholm in May 1962. He was a member of the Salvation Army and his singing career also included appearances at Covent Garden, Sadlers Wells and the Edinburgh Festival. Kevin was a member of the choir when Arthur Martin died under tragic circumstances in 1960. The choir continued for a time under the leadership of Maureen Sands, who had been an

accompanist with the choir. But the death of this remarkable teacher brought to a close this chapter in the history of choral music in general and Ulster boy sopranos in particular. Arthur Martin was greatly mourned by those who knew him.

The
Manchester Cathedral Boys

Manchester Cathedral Choir - Harlech, 1931

Each of The Better Land CDs has a strong northern flavour and three of the boys featured were members of Manchester Cathedral Choir, trained by Archibald Wayet Wilson and his assistant, Norman Cocker. The Cathedral itself dates back over six hundred years and is built in the Perpendicular Gothic style, typified by its tall windows and flat fan-vaulted ceilings. Although it sustained a direct hit in the Manchester Blitz of December 1940, the shattered windows acted as a safety valve, releasing the force of the explosion- so that much of the structure remained undamaged. Unfortunately many of the written archives detailing the history of the choir were destroyed but, thankfully, the Chapter records were recovered and these I was able to study.

From the year 1421 the Cathedral statutes provide for four singing boys and although the number of choristers was increased in Victorian times, special status is still afforded to these 'foundation' boys. A minute of 1911 sets the payment of two of these boys at £10 per annum, the others receiving £5 and £3 respectively. In the early days of the last century the choir school, which took day-boys from as far away as Southport and Bolton, used various premises, all of them inconvenient because of problems of noise or distance from the Cathedral. Twice daily the boys would face a long walk in procession under police escort.

Later, in the early 1930s, a purpose-built school was opened in the Cathedral Yard comprising three classrooms and a refectory and, although there were no playground or games facilities, the boys were allowed to use the yard of the nearby Chetham's Hospital for recreational purposes. Educational standards at the school had been deemed unsatisfactory for some time and did not improve until the Revd

George Skeet was appointed headmaster in 1926.

Little is recorded about the standard of music at the Cathedral during the tenure as organist of Sir Sydney Nicholson, but his relations with the canons were not good due perhaps to his 'advanced' ideas. In 1917 the Chapter agreed that he 'be informed that hymn tunes which are not known to the congregation shall only be introduced in the Cathedral services with great discretion' and that 'he be desired to arrange in future for the use of Anglican Chants in the place of Gregorian Chants in the services.'

Following his departure to Westminster Abbey in 1918 the canons and Dean-elect, Prebendary William Shuckburgh Swayne, offered the post of organist to Dr Dykes-Bower (who declined the position) before appointing Dr Wayet Wilson, charging him with the task of restoring previous high musical standards. Wilson had wanted to appoint his own sub-organist but the Chapter insisted on seeing all applications and invited the hitherto unknown Norman Cocker for interview. One of the canons, the Revd Victor Dams, wrote an interesting account of Cocker's interview:

'Canon Scott [Acting Dean]: "I notice that you did not take your degree at Oxford. Why was that, Mr Cocker?"
Cocker: "I was sent down."
Canon Scott: "Sent down, Mr Cocker?"
Cocker: "I didn't do any work."

They appointed him on the spot at a salary of £175! Cocker seems to have been a wise choice and he had a great influence on the lives of many of the choristers, eventually succeeding Wilson as Organist in 1943, and holding the post until his death ten years later. A popular man with a charismatic personality he may have been unique amongst cathedral organists in that he was also organist at six cinemas. His obituary in *The Manchester Guardian* added that he was a fine cook, a brilliant conjuror and also a designer of stage-sets!

In 1924 the controversial Dr Hewlett Johnson was appointed Dean and from the outset took a personal interest in the welfare of the choir boys, resolving to improve the conditions at the school. He seems to have gained the support of Mr Craddock, a senior lay clerk and singing master to the boys. After George Skeet was appointed headmaster, the Chapter ruled in 1927 that no-one be permitted to cane the choir boys except the headmaster; and any bad behaviour to be reported to him 'on a form'. Certainly 'no disciplinary action of any kind [was to be taken] by the organist, precentor or headmaster within the Cathedral precincts.'

Very soon educational standards were raised and in 1929 Inspectors reported the boys were 'courteous and well-behaved'. Choir camps were arranged under the Dean's personal supervision and Mrs Cherry Johnstone tells us of the camp at Prestatyn in 1929 when a boy was swept out to sea by currents. Hewlett Johnson, in full clerical clothes as always, dived in, pulled the boy out and gave life-saving drill for a considerable time. The boy was almost given up for dead when he sneezed and opened his eyes. The other boys ran to the village to get help and the two were driven back to Manchester.

The Dean also encouraged the formation of an additional voluntary choir of gentlemen and boys to help out at Evensong on Sundays and at special ser, vices, and he wrote many years later that it was 'nearly one hundred in number and splendidly marshalled and trained by Mr Craddock.'

Robert Duncan Peel

In 1926, the Dean was approached by the British Broadcasting Company (as the BBC was then known) with a view to relaying a service from the Cathedral on the first Sunday of every other month.

The Sub-Dean, Canon Scott, entered a strong protest but he was overruled and several services were broadcast during that year, the fees being given to local hospitals. It was during one of these broadcasts that the engineers heard fifteen-year-old John Bonner, whose voice they described to Hewlett Johnson as 'the best treble voice in England'.

As a result of this publicity, John Bonner and thirteen-year-old Duncan Peel became the first Manchester choir boys to make gramophone records. Peel was born in 1914 and entered the choir in 1921. In 1927, the Columbia record company was looking for a boy soprano to equal Ernest Lough, whose recordings had just been issued by HMV. Their recording van was brought to the Cathedral where the two boys were recorded in September of that year. Peel's song was not entirely satisfactory and it was hoped to re-record it at a subsequent session. Unfortunately his voice brok soon after the recording, so the record was issued in 1928 with an organ solo by Wilson on the reverse. Peel later completed organ studies at Durham Cathedral and in 1933 was appointed Vicar Choral at Armagh Cathedral, eventually becoming organist of Shankill Parish Church, Lurgan, where he remained until his death in 1999.

John Bonner's recording of Haydn's With vedure clad (made at the same sessions as Peel's record) was judged excellent and it was issued before Peel's early in 1928.   In those days the majority of choir boys were the sons of working class parents and John was no exception. He was born in Manchester in May 1912 and even as a small boy at the Municipal school he possessed an outstanding voice; the teachers used to stand him on a chair and let him sing to the class! His great-grandfather had been a bass at the cathedral but his mother was reluctant to allow John to become a chorister.

John Bonner

Mrs Bonner, like many Anglicans in those days, objected to ritual and had been alarmed when one of the family had converted to Catholicism. The Dean, however, was as charming as he was brave and put her mind entirely at rest, giving his assurance that the boy would not be subjected to 'unwholesome' influences. John became a cathedral chorister at the age of ten, his solo career taking off as a result of the BBC broadcasts and because of his first recording with all the subsequent publicity. *The Manchester Guardian* commented that '[Ernest Lough] has a remarkable voice. But he sings with two distinct registers, the upper notes sounding like a velvety-toned flute, but the middle and lower tones ringing with a hard chesty production of the clarinet type. However, Manchester Cathedral, a few Sundays ago, introduced a boy whose voice was a delight. He sang a long and difficult solo without the slightest signs of chesty tone, all one even exquisite quality, beautifully blended.'

John went on to record eight more songs during the period 1928/1929 when he would have been nearly seventeen years old. On the occasion of his recording of Braga's Angels' Serenade the orchestra had difficulty with the ensemble. After several rehearsals John asked the conductor for his baton saying: 'Let me have a go - after all, I've got to sing it!' The conductor apparently gave him 'a filthy look' but handed over the baton and John stood and conducted the orchestra as he sang, making the published recording at the first attempt.

In addition to recordings in London there were concert appearances throughout the north of England. A typical report would mention huge crowds packing the halls. *The Oldham Evening Chronicle* reported that 'Master Bonner once again succeeded in captivating his audience. He has a sweet natural voice of much expression, with splendid enunciation.' A year later, in January 1930 when he was almost eighteen, John was the principal attraction at the La Scala Kinema, Hollingwood, which was packed and many turned away disappointed. 'In the dim light of the theatre he appeared far away and it seemed as if his voice could not possibly carry. But he could be heard clearly and certainly deserves his fame. During his rendering of Liddle's *Abide with me,* many members of the audience were visibly affected. Encores were numerous and the boy responded freely.'

It was reported that John's rich and expressive voice could move concert audiences to tears, and crowds would flock to the Cathedral when it was known he was singing a solo there. Years later, Dr. Hewlett Johnson was to recall that 'Bonner was outstanding. When he rose to sing his solo in the Children's Service, the shuffling of hundreds of feet ceased'. The Dean sometimes took him to sing at 'posh' functions from which he would return home the following day. He would also be asked round to the Deanery to sing to special guests, after which he would be given a fine meal and put to bed by the servants.

John was devoted to Hewlett Johnson, whom he regarded as his friend and mentor, and to the sub organist, Norman Cocker. But relations with the choirmaster, Mr Wilson, were not good. 'He always had it in for me,' John later told his wife. On one occasion, he ran away from the choir and refused to go back until the Dean had driven round to his house in his motor car with a large hydrangea to plead with him to return!

John sang as a boy at the cathedral for seven years until what was described at the time as 'an incipient roughness' put an end to his days as a soprano soloist'. Three years later Hewlett Johnson suggested he re-commence voice-training and he returned to the Cathedral as deputy bass. In 1935, at the age of 22, he was interviewed by Sir Walter Alcock, the organist at Salisbury Cathedral, securing the position of bass lay-vicar.

When he became engaged to a Sheffield girl, John moved to Lincoln Minster and, in the late 1930's, became musical director of several musical societies in the county. Around that time Norman Cocker composed arrangements of Tate's *Somewhere a Voice is Calling* and Godard's *Angels Guard Thee* for John to sing, dubbing his baritone voice onto his earlier soprano recording of the same works. This was a new idea and it was to be many years before a similar duet was recorded by Aled Jones.

When war broke out John joined the RAF and, in India, became a member of Ralph Reader's Gang Show and also broadcast on All-India Radio. After the war he returned to Lincoln, where he formed the 'John Bonner Concert Orchestra'. Following their marriage, he moved with his wife, Mabel, to Sheffield where they ran a newsagent's shop for many years. He was director of the Sheffield Teachers' Operatic Society until shortly before his death in 1979.

Fifty years after making his first record, John had made a private recording of the song he had sung many years before at the funeral of Dr HewlettJohnson's wife in Canterbury Cathedral. Introducing *There is no Death,* he said: 'You have heard the boy soprano and the same voice ten years later. Now here is the same voice fifty years later.' He sat at the piano and sang for the last time. After he died the Sheffield press paid tribute to his 'infectious exuberance and enthusiasm. His training as a boy and adult chorister in Manchester and Lincoln, together with his wartime direction of an orchestra in India, could well have fitted him for a successful professional career, but in music he preferred to associate himself with the "amateurs" of this world for whom he had the greatest devotion. In 1929, Hewlett Johnson had written in *The Manchester Guardian,* 'People a hundred years hence will be deeply touched by this boy's voice.'

Shortly before my publisher's deadline, news came to us of the final soloist of the choir to feature in the series: Gordon Carter, who recorded Mendelssohn's *O for the wings of a dove* whilst princpal soloist in 1934. He was born in 1918 of a musical family (his father was a professional violinist) and began his singing career as a chorister at Oldham Parish Church. There, the organist, Dr Cooper, realising the boy's potential, took him for an audition at the Cathedral, where he was accepted, and joined the choir in 1928. Like his cousin, John Bonner, before him, Gordon soon rose to the ranks of soloist and fulfilled many engagements in Manchester and beyond, at the theatres and cinemas which were available for sacred concerts onSundays due to the strict censoring of secular materil performed then.

John Bonner and Gordon Carter, 1938

The timing of Gordon's recording was fortuitous as, only a few days after making the discs for the 'Rex' company in London, his voice broke and he had to leave the choir. Speaking to reporters in Manchester, Gordon thought it unlikely he would sing again. 'It is unusual', he said, 'for a good juvenile voice to turn into an equally good adult voice.' He was by this time sixteen and intended to remain at school and study for the Ministry, but the war put paid to his ambitions and his wartime experiences led him to believe that he could not in conscience be ordained.

However, although he did not train as an adult singer, he took a degree and became a schoolmaster, eventually becoming Schools' Music Advisor for Gloucestershire. In later years he wrote many educational books and taught singing and piano privately. His talent and training at Manchester had given him a life-long passion for music and he possessed the gift of communicating that love to the children whom he taught to sing. Gordon believed the traditional 'head-tone' sound should continue to be taught and was concerned that children should not pick up what he described as a 'guttural tone'.

He continued teaching until shortly before his death in 2004 and, over the years, ran residential singing courses and brought many choirs together to perform major works, sometimes accompanied by the Hallé Orchestra. Three of Gordon Carter's soprano records were unpublished but he retained copies of them. The search for the three recorded soloists of Manchester Cathedral has come to an end and it is satisfying that we have, through the help of so many people, been able to piece together and tell for the first time the story of this choir and its soloists.

The Northern Lights

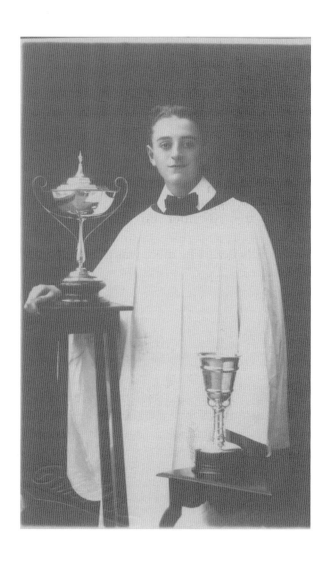

Master Frederick Firth

The North of England boasts a fine musical tradition and many a boy soprano competed at the famous Blackpool Music Festival, which was one of the most prestigious in Britain before the Second World War. The tonic sol–fa method of music notation (introduced in the nineteenth century by John Curwen) had enabled people with little experience to read music atsight in any key, and this had resulted in a growing number of choral societies.

Such was the musical background of Kenneth Purves. And it is thanks to Colin Charnley and Douglas Carrington (who both saw my appeal for information in *Cathedral Music*) that I am able to relate the life of this 'Wonder Boy Singer' as he was described at the time. Through their good offices Ken Purves, shortly before he died, was persuaded towrite an account of his career as a boy soprano, and from his beautifully written 'copperplate' memoir we quote from time to time.

Kenneth Purves was born in New Longton, Lancashire, in December 1911, the son of a master tailor in Oreston. His father was an amateur musician who ran his own choir and his mother had a soprano voice of solo quality. They had both sung under the baton of Sir Henry Wood.

'You must understand that I was born to sing,' Ken wrote, 'and I arrived [in this world] to the sound of a Glee Party going on in the drawing-room below.' It was soon evident that young Ken possessed a fine singing voice himself and, just before hiseleventh birthday, his parents decided that he should have lessons. He was placed under the tutelage of Tom Wright, who lived in the adjacent village, and in 1923, about two weeks after his twelfth birthday, Ken made his solo debut. 'A couple of weeks after that I sang *Come unto Him* and *I know that my Redeemer liveth* in a performance of Handel's *Messiah*, my mother taking the remainder of the soprano solos. Dad conducted the augmented chapel choirs. The following year, mother stood down completely in my favour.'

In 1925 Ken made the first of three appearances at the Blackpool Music Festival in the Open Boy Soprano Class and also in the Chorister Class, gaining a first and a second. He was to repeat this in 1926 and again at the age of fifteen in 1927, taking first place in each class. It was thought that his voice would not last until the following year when he would be almost seventeen, so he did not enter. 'However, I did go along to listen and as it happens I was singing better than ever and the standard of the competition was lower.'

By this time Ken was in demand, singing at concerts and church services each weekend and travelling as far south as London as well as throughout the North of England with an evangelist named Tom Holland.

Master Kenneth Purves

'We would travel on a Saturday to give a concert followed by two services - both with solos - on the Sunday, rounding off the day with a concert of sacred music in the evening. On the Monday afternoon a performance in a local works canteen would be followed by a concert in the evening. We would then travel back overnight or on the Tuesday morning.' Ken had left school by this time and was learning his father's trade, often being seen around the shop from quite an early age.

Ken revelled in the vast audiences who came to hear him sing. He remembered that 'at Tunstall in the Potteries we had over 2000 people at each concert in the Methodist chapel and at Roker we had a marquee on the beach and packed in similar audiences throughout the weekend - great days!'

It was as a direct result of his success at the Blackpool Festival in 1927 that he was first invited to broadcast from the Manchester Station of the BBC. He was then engaged as soloist with a choir of 600 boys to sing at a concert in the splendid St. George's Hall, Liverpool. 'I will never forget it or the indescribable moment when there was dead silence as I finished singing and then the most tremendous burst of applause!'

In 1927 Arthur Homewood, the advertising manager of The Gramophone Company (better known as HMV), tried to arrange a contract for the boy. The company was unwilling to enter into any agreement as they considered the commercial success of Ernest Lough's recordings was unlikely to be repeated. But they did agree to make a 'one-off' pressing for Ken's family, and Mendelssohn's *Hear ye Israel* was recorded in the first floor studio of the Queen's Hall in Langham Place (sadly destroyed in the London Blitz by incendiary bombs in May 1941).

'I made the record on my way home to Preston after a concert in Swindon. We ran through the piece several times to get the right length for the 12-inch wax master. At the end of the recording, the lady accompanist forgetting the disc was still turning leaned over to me and whispered "Well done!" and her voice was captured on the wax.' Just one or two copies were pressed and these were thought to have been discarded though one was unexpectedly discovered by Colin Charnley on a market stall in Preston in 1959, and thanks to him we were able to feature it on *The Better Land* CD series.

Perhaps hearing this 'demonstration' disc, the Vocalion Gramophone Company offered to feature Ken on their new 8-inch 'Broadcast' records, which were sold for one shilling and three pence at gramophone shops across the country. Ken learnt some of the music, including Attwood's *Come Holy Ghost,* en route to London on the Fylde Coast Express, which reached Euston in those days 3 hours 37 minutes after leaving Blackpool. Six discs were made in two days at the Stoll Theatre, Kingsway, in the spring of 1928. On the first day of recording Ken was accompanied by an organ and mixed-voice quartet but the following morning he was joined in Mendelssohn's duet *I waited for the Lord* by James Duggan and the Eton College Chapel Choir. One of the records from the first session, *Hear my prayer,* eventually went on to sell over 339,000 copies, although Ken never saw any royalties. 'I was paid a flat fee of ten guineas plus expenses and given a portable gramophone,' he explained!

Ken went on to sing until he was well over seventeen but after that his musical career was completely forgotten. Douglas Carrington traced him in 1985 when Ken admitted that he did not possess nor had he heard any of his records in over forty years. He even had to borrow a cassette player from a neighbour in order to play copies of his discs provided by Colin Charnley! Sadly, he died fourteen years before the discs were properly remastered and featured on *The Better Land.*

Kenneth Purves became a master tailor, and

ran his business until retirement in the early 1980s. He lived to see his son, Peter, rise to fame, first in the cult television programme, *Dr Who*, and later as one of the all-time favourite presenters of the children's magazine programme, *Blue Peter*.

Contemporaneous with the career of Kenneth Purves was that of Frederick Firth, who was born and brought up in Morecambe, Lancashire. He was trained by his uncle Mark Stoddart, a local music master, and began to take part in competitive festivals in 1925 at the age of twelve. It is interesting to read in his scrapbook of his improved marks over the next four years when he competed at festivals held in some very small towns including Colne and Millom as well as appearing at Morecambe and Blackpool. By the age of fourteen, Fred's voice was mature and attracting high praise, and at the Blackpool Festival in 1928, at the age of fifteen, he was awarded the seemingly impossible 101 marks out of 100 for sight singing by the adjudicator, Geoffrey Shaw. 'I believe this is the first time [this has ever happened]' Shaw wrote, 'but I see no reason why the extra mark should not be given.' The sum total of Master Firth's successes at Blackpool over the

Master Frederick Firth

years was four firsts and two cups - one for boys' solo singing (under sixteen) and the other for church choir boys.

In July 1927 the BBC, through the good offices of Sir Edward Elgar, invited Fred to make a broadcast from their Manchester station. It was to be the first of many and he was immediately engaged for *Children's Hour* and for a broadcast from Birmingham, for which he was paid a fee of one guinea. Acting on advice from the BBC, Fred's parents accepted a recording contract from British Brunswick, turning down an offer from HMV who, although it would have required a formal test session, would have paid royalties. Brunswick increased its offer from £45 to £50 for four titles and it is not difficult to see why this was accepted.

The company was known to produce much better quality discs than HMV, who at the time used hard-wearing but consequently very noisy shellac, and it is interesting to note that an offer of a test by the Vocalion Company was not thought worthy of consideration by Fred's father! In December 1928 Fred sang at the Tower Ballroom, Blackpool, and a reviewer wrote: 'the Lancashire boy with the golden voice quickly won all hearts by his simplicity of manner and ease of delivery.' He received six guineas for the performance.

Frederick Firth continued to sing until he was nearly sixteen years of age. 'I went on a lot longer than the average boy, perhaps too long. Because I was so highly trained I was able to retain my singing voice well into my teens. In fact I did begin to train my baritone voice before I gave up as a boy soprano,' he added, 'but I was told by Stanford Robinson that in continuing so long as a boy I had sacrificed the prospects of having a fine adult solo voice. I still think it was a price worth paying.'

When the idea of producing a CD of boy sopranos was first discussed, Martin Carson introduced me to Mr Firth, then aged eighty-eight and living in retirement in Norwich. After he had related his story to us, displaying his cups and albums with his wife by his side, he asked me to play a tape of his recordings. We then sat in silence as Fred closed his eyes, sat back and silently mouthed the words he had committed to wax seventy years previously. 'That's a difficult phrase,taken in just one breath!' he would interject, or: 'the words are very good here!'

Frederick died soon after our visit, but not before he had lived to see the reissue of his recordings on CD and enjoyed the subsequent publicity in the press and on local radio. One of his records was included at his funeral service. It was our meeting with him that fuelled our determination to trace the other boys who were to feature on *The Better Land* series of CD's.

We had given up all hope of uncovering information about Raymond Kinsey, who features on several of the *The Better Land* CD's. For many years, for reasons I cannot explain, I had mistakenly believed that he had been a soloist at Manchester Cathedral and had included what little information I had in that chapter. However, a few weeks before my publisher's deadline, Sonita Cox at EMI found a contract in the archives dating from 1933 signed by Lucy Ann Kinsey, the boy's mother, and giving an address in Girlington, Bradford. From that information Brian Pearson was able to trace the marriage of a Harold Kinsey and Lucy Jameson whose son, Raymond, was born in Bradford in 1920. He was just twelve when made his first record. The critic C.M. Crabtree was particularly impressed and, writing in *The Gramophone*, said, 'if all boy soprano records were as good as [this] they would be really welcome. Handel's *Rejoice greatly* and *Let the bright seraphim* are especially suitable for boys who are, as Kinsey is, equal to them.'

The inadvisability of relying exclusively on press reports to compile the account of a person's life and career is borne out in Raymond's case. After applying for Raymond's death certificate I was able, following a difficult search, to contact his daughter, Rose, and she told me her father's story with the help of scrapbooks compiled by Raymond's cousin, Eunice Flint, who had kept a contemporaneous account of the boy's singing career.

Raymond Kinsey was brought up by his widowed mother and grandparents in Girlington, where, at the age of eight, he joined St. Philip's Church choir. His choirmaster, Mr A. C. Scott, noticed his considerable natural talent for singing and entered him in the prestigious competitive music festivals. A note made by Raymond in the margin of a scrapbook just before his death confirms Eunice's statement that 'his amazing technique was, like his voice, a gift. Even though he won almost every singing competition he entered, his tuition consisted of no more than one very brief weekly lesson at his choirmaster's house for a fee of 1/- per session.' She added that 'he would make any excuse to avoid practice and was clever enough to do so with the greatest regularity'.

Raymond had taken piano lessons from his cousin and this 'gave him the little knowledge he needed to display his gift. Once he had sung a song through, he could negotiate the difficulties with a facility and purity that even his recordings can never quite convey.'

Raymond competed in no fewer than fifteen festivals and following his success at the Blackpool

Festival in 1932, (where he was awarded the same silver cup won some years previously by Frederick Firth), he was offered an audition to record at HMV's new studio in Abbey Road, London, where in January 1933 he recorded Handel's *Let the bright Seraphim* and *Rejoice greatly* with piano accompaniment.

A few weeks later he recorded these again with an orchestra for commercial production, members of the press being invited to watch the recording session. As a result, attempts were made by the media to invent a story of the Kinsey family's financial difficulties, of Raymond's hard practice and expensive tuition. 'In fact nothing could have been further from the truth,' Eunice wrote, 'but to listen to Raymond's records even the experts could be forgiven for believing at least the latter part to be true.' The BBC presenter and reviewer Christopher Stone (who attended the recording session) remarked in *The Daily Express* that 'judging by his complete assurance in front of the microphone ... and by his undaunted attack ... we have here a boy who may well enrich the record library with singing that has never been equalled for effortless art by any of his generation.' Other newspapers, including the *Daily Herald* reported the event, embellishing details and fabricating a story that he had been too small to reach the microphone. Raymond later commented that this was 'absolute nonsense' and that most of the reports 'did not contain a word of truth.'

Several London newspapers also took the story, including *The Daily Mirror*, which reported that Raymond's mother had returned to work to ensure 'the means for having her son's voice properly developed by expert tuition.' In fact, Raymond's lessons comprised, as we have already stated, of a single

Daily Sketch added that 'Raymond's fine singing ruined the first attempt to record him: that, when he began to sing, members of the London Symphony Orchestra had been so astonished that they had stopped playing and the record was ruined'. These and other myths were, much to Raymond's annoyance, perpetuated for many years. However it is agreed that the description in *The Daily Sketch* of his being a 'coloratura soprano' is indeed accurate. 'The astonishing ease, certainty and clarity with which he takes the most florid runs make one exclaim "Can this be a boy?" His voice has a timbre and fullness of a prima donna's, and is as flexible and as agile as that of a world-famed diva.'

Raymond was to record twice more - in April and in September 1933 when he was thirteen years old. His songs received excellent reviews, particularly in respect of his expression and ability to communicate his deep feeling for and involvement with the music. The reviewer Herman Klein noted in *The Gramophone* that 'there is in this boy's voice a dark, rich colour and a beauty of texture that are quite exceptional. The same adjective applies to his breath-control, the evenness of his scale, the depth and maturity of his expressive power.'

Mr Scott, his choirmaster, believed Raymond's voice would last another two years , but it began to break towards the end of 1933, necessitating the cancellation of many engagements including a forthcoming BBC contract. 'No-one would believe my voice was breaking,' Raymond wrote, 'but I did finally convince them. By that time singing had become a nightmare' He left St. Philip's Church choir in April 1934 and although he continued his musical interests he never sang again. By the age of nineteen he had been the leader of three dance bands in which he played the tenor saxophone. During the war he served in the RAF as a Flight Lieutenant involved in the teaching of 'Blind Approach' technique. In 1946, by now married with two small children, he took up photography and film making and embarked on a career as a producer, eventually running his own company making mainly missionary films, based at CMS off Fleet Street.

The story of Raymond's career was very much one of his fulfilling his considerable natural talents and furthering his many interests in life. As a boy soprano, his virtually untrained voice was all the more remarkable in that it was possessed by one so young. As a twelve-year old he had sung with the expression and control of a boy in his late teens.

After he retired, Raymond returned to Yorkshire where he died in Bingley in 1997. It is satisfying to be able to complete this chapter with his story which very nearly was not included. 'He would have loved to have been here', his daughter, Rose said to me, 'to see the fruits of your work and to hear his records re-issued in *The Better Land* series.'

Master Raymond Kinsey

The Boys of Music Hall, Stage & Light Entertainment

National Player-Piano Week
March 6th-10th

GRAHAM PAYN
THE BOY SOPRANO
AT
HARRODS
Daily 3.30 p.m.

Victorians loved the Music Hall: putting a boy with a good soprano voice on the stage was usually a sure recipe for success. Attempting to trace the earliest mention of the term 'boy soprano' has been a lengthy task and research is far from complete. The earliest traced mention of such a singer on stage was of Joseph Howard, composer and vaudeville performer, who appeared in St. Louis in 1878/9 at the age of eleven billed as 'Master Joseph, Boy Soprano'. In England in 1894, 'Master George Elliott, the wonderful boy soprano' appeared at the Circus of Varieties on Newgate in Rochdale after having achieved success in America. Elliott later found fame in London as the 'Chocolate-Coloured Coon' but whether his earlier designation originated in the USA or Britain is not clear. The origins of the term are shrouded in mystery and the whole subject of boy actors/singers appearing on stage from Shakespearian times through the critical changes after the Restoration of Charles II in 1660 (when men and boys were banned from playing female parts and women first allowed to appear) is a neglected area of social history.

Many well known entertainers also began their careers as boy singers - Al Jolson, Arthur Askey, Charles Hawtrey and Clifford Adams, for example. Hawtrey had made records with one of the few girls to have recorded, Evelyn Griffiths; and Cliff Adams (of 'Sing Something Simple' fame) always denied he was the self-same boy soprano who had recorded such sentimental numbers as *Ashamed of his poor old dad*, but shortly before his death he revealed the truth to the broadcaster Frank Wappatt.

Wappatt also 'discovered' the truth about Master Joe Petersen, otherwise known as Mary O'Rourke, who was born in 1913. Her uncle, Ted Stebbings, had been a boy soprano (singing under the name of Edward Frisby) and had trained his son in similar fashion. But when the boy's voice broke he looked for a 'boy' whose career would continue and persuaded his niece, then aged eighteen, to cross dress and assume the rôle of 'Master' Joe Petersen. The result was utterly convincing, although, as time passed, and Master Petersen did not 'grow up', many became suspicious. The larger record companies were not interested and the BBC refused to play any of 'his' records, issued on the 'Rex' label.

Petersen's voice was remarkably boy-like with a contralto quality, and Mary O'Rourke could certainly have made a name for herself in her own right had she not been trapped in a boy's costume. It is well-known that television led to the demise of the Music Hall after the last war, and Mary, like so many other artistes, fell on hard times. She last appeared as Joe Petersen at the Metropole, Glasgow in 1963 but by this time she had taken to drink and died a year later, thirty years after making her first recording. Frank Wappatt found her simple grave and tells the story movingly in his book 'Master Joe Petersen'.

We pick up our story in 1929 when Graham Payn – a twelve-year-old boy from Johannesburg who had just won three singing competitions – persuaded his mother to bring him to London. 'I told her I wanted to be in the films', he explained. 'I wanted to be like Douglas Fairbanks!'

Graham had been taught singing by his mother who was an excellent musician. In London he found plenty of work on stage at cinemas throughout the capital, singing between films and often giving four or five shows a day. British Pathé often concluded its twice-weekly newsreel with a light-hearted item and a boy soprano was sometimes featured. Graham, possibly the first of these boys, was filmed three times during 1931-32 and these brief excerpts provide a unique insight into his style of performance. Amongst other boys to feature in the nineteen thirties were Iwan Davies, who has already been mentioned, Denis Armand Gonet (who had a remarkable and true tenor voice at the age of thirteen), and Frank Bird, who was filmed in 1939.

Graham Payn went on to appear in review with stars like Elsie and Doris Waters, the Western Brothers and Tommy Handley, to name just a few. 'I would appear in Eton suit and stiff collar and sing my heart out', he recalled

Later Graham was to become Noel Coward's life-long friend and companion, meeting him for the first time when he auditioned at the Adelphi Theatre in 1932 for *Words and Music*, Coward's latest review. 'My mother told me that, as I would get just a few minutes to prove myself, I had better sing and dance at the same time, so that's what I did, and sang *Nearer my God to Thee* while doing a tap-dance on the stage! When I had finished, Noel said in his clipped tones, "We must have that kid in the show!" ' Graham started in the show by earning a handsome fee of five pounds per week for playing a beggar boy singing to a cinema queue. 'I really threw myself into it, behaving like a whirling dervish until Noel stopped me and said , "Graham, we know what a great little artiste you are but the boy you're playing would stand quite still and just sing". So I did stand - like a rock!'

In common with so many other boys of the period Graham didn't know at what time he should stop singing. 'When I was nearly sixteen my mother said that my voice should have broken and she took me to a doctor who told me that my voice <u>had</u> actually broken some time before and that I was singing in what he described as "head tones". He told me to stop at once'. Given that advice, Graham decided to 'call it a day' before he ruined his voice. He cancelled six weeks' work and returned to South Africa where he attended a stage and dance school. After the war, when he was beginning to make a name for himself, Noel Coward asked him to appear in his new review *Sigh No More*, writing the song *Matelot* especially for him. After Coward's death in 1973 Graham remained in their home in Switzerland to run the estate. After hearing about the release of *The Better Land* CDs, he was thrilled to think of his records being reissued. 'After all,' he concluded, 'everyone who heard me sing on stage must be dead!'

I began searching for Master Leslie Day in the late 1970s after discovering his recording of Harford-Marshall's *I hear you calling me* in a second-hand record shop in Sheffield. It was when I heard his somewhat haunting voice for the first time that I conceived the idea of compiling a CD of boy soprano recordings. At the time of writing, twenty-five years later, little more is known about this boy who

The wonder voice of 14-year-old

LESLIE DAY

has made him a " star " even when so young. He is not one of those untried, unpractised boy singers often heard, but he uses his voice with feeling and sympathy. He sang in the choir of St. Barnabas, Hackney. His " discovery " led to his introduction to London Pavilion audiences, who clamour nightly for encores. He was introduced to wireless audiences on May 13th, proving a huge success with listeners. Hear this wonder record—so beautifully sung.

FOR YOU ALONE.

I HEAR YOU CALLING ME.

Master LESLIE DAY, Boy Soprano.

Record No. DB1122 (2/6)

EXCLUSIVE TO COLUMBIA.

inspired my search: just two or three scraps of information have been discovered, gleaned from theatre bills, a Columbia advert and a letter in the EMI Archives.   One suspects that there would be a remarkable story to tell had we been able to trace him.

Leslie Day had been a chorister at St. Barnabas's church, Hackney and in 1933, aged fourteen, he was 'discovered' and thrust into the limelight during a broadcast in the BBC National Programme. He then appeared for some considerable time on stage at the London Pavilion, Piccadilly.   He went on to sing in two short films, *Television Follies English* in 1933 (singing Bingham – Malloy's *Love's old sweet song*), and *Musical Medley Mancunian* in 1935.   He would by that time have been nearly sixteen.   Unfortunately both films have been lost: a letter in the EMI archives gives his manager as Lilly Denville but nothing further is known about him or his career.

Steffani and his Silver Songsters must be mentioned at this point as several recorded soloists emerged from this remarkable singing troupe.   Those featured on *The Better Land*, Dai Thomas, Morris Stevens and Cyril Lewis, were trained by Steffani, although Lewis was not a member of the group when he made his record.

Frederick William Wisker was born in March 1904, at Beccles in Suffolk.and demonstrated early musical talent – he was caught busking in the street outside his house at the age of three! He adopted the stage name Freddie Northcoat and began his professional career as pianist and singer. By 1934 he had formed two choirs - 'The Sixteen Singing Scholars' and 'The Abbey Singers', and had assumed the stage name of Arturo Steffani.   Around 1935 he picked the best boys from the two groups and formed Steffani and his Silver Songsters. Fred and Frank Cox joined

Steffani's troupe after he turned up on their door step in Wales offering them music lessons, beautiful white suits and guitars plus five shillings if they would join. The twins told me that they danced for him on the mat!

The group originally comprised twenty-one boys aged between twelve and fourteen years and it is thought that most originated from the Tiger Bay area of Cardiff. Steffani took the boys to London, finding lodgings for them in the Tottenham Court Road.

The main act was introduced by a 'cathedral scene'. The stage-curtains would open, revealing stained-glass windows through which the sun shone. The show would usually begin with the boys singing Ketèlbey's *In a Monastery Garden*, Steffani conducting from the orchestra pit. Then, dressed all in their silver and white costumes, Fred and Frank, known as 'The Silver Twins', would perform a dance routine. Cowboy numbers would then follow!

The boys sang with many of the well-known stars of the day in theatres throughout the country and made a number of recordings in the mid to late '30s. In 1936 they even appeared in a film, *Dodging the Dole*. There were also broadcasts for the BBC and a five-week tour of Denmark, Norway and Sweden early in 1939. The schedule was always tough, performing at least twice daily six days a week before moving on to the next town. Steffani's other choir, 'The Harlem Pages', comprised a group of twelve blacked-up boys who sometimes appeared on the same bill.

The curtain came down on *The Silver Songsters* in 1947. Although most of the boys left show business when their voices broke, some remained and a few became quite famous, including Norman Vaughan, The Cox Twins and the whistler, Ronnie Ronalde.

Although Robert Harris could hardly be described as a music hall artiste his story fits well into

this chapter. Robert's recording of Schubert's *Who is Sylvia?* and Barrie - Coates' *Birdsong at Eventide* were featured in volumes 1 and 3 of *The Better Land* series, but it was only after an appeal in *Evergreen* magazine that we managed to trace him. In November 2000, I visited Robert in his Cheshire home and he was pleased to relate his boyhood experiences.

He was born in March 1920 and, from the age of nine, had sung in the choir of St. Ethelburga's Church, St.Leonard's-on-Sea.

Master Robert Harris

Until the age of twelve he was a pupil of Miss Lilian Cordell and cycled eight miles from his home in St. Leonard's to Hastings to attend his lessons. 'I would spend the first ten minutes of every lesson trying to out-breathe her, and she was no small lady!' he told me. The Headmaster of Downsmeade School, Eastbourne, Mr Wilson, noticed Robert's well developed voice and offered him a free education in return for singing in the choir of Holy Trinity church where he was choirmaster.

Robert therefore left home to be a boarder at the school. 'Looking back at it now, I am surprised my mother let me go,' he commented, 'but it was a marvellous opportunity'. Between 1933 and 1936, he took first prize in the Brighton Music Festival, and was also successful at Hastings and Stratford. On one occasion, he was presented with a silver watch, and after winning the Brighton Festival three years in a row he was allowed to keep the cup!

In 1934 Robert was invited by the BBC to sing in the programme *Grand Hotel*, which was broadcast in those pre-war years from Eastbourne (though during the war, when the hotel was occupied by the Ministry of Defence, it was relayed from venues elsewhere). As already mentioned, several of the boys featured in this book took part in the programme at various times and all Robert's Parlophone records were made in that famous lounge accompanied by the Palm Court Orchestra.

'I had to stand in front of a cone-like microphone which was shaped like a dunce's cap and I was told to take a pace back just before hitting a high note, and then stand forward again in order to avoid overloading the system. Sometimes we had to speed up a song or slow it down in order to fit it onto the wax disc in the van parked outside the hotel!' Robert, who continued singing until the age of seventeen, got time off school to pursue his career and often appeared in concerts in the south of England and in London, including an appearance with George Thalben-Ball.

'My speaking voice had broken by then but I stopped before my singing voice broke, as I can remember it becoming a little more difficult towards the end. Miss Cordell had taught me to throw the voice up into the back of the head which was easy to do. I had a very good range with a break so I could get power in the lower register. A choirboy wouldn't have that break - he would produce a head-tone throughout the range. It was difficult to sing smooth-ly through the break at around C and I always listen for that on my records.'

Robert Harris, on left, with school friends

Sadly most of Robert's close school friends pic-tured with him were killed in the war. In 1940 he joined the Royal Engineers and served until 1946, leaving the army with the rank of Captain. 'After the war I trained part-time at the Guildhall School of Music, but I could have done with a couple of extra notes at both ends of the baritone range. I then realised I would never again be as good as I had been earlier.'

Robert embarked upon a distinguished career in industry, which took him abroad. He was involved with others in creating the Nigerian Ports Authority and in 1960 became Assistant Manager of the Manchester Ship Canal Company. Retiring aged sixty-five he was able to add the OBE to his proud col-lection of boyhood singing cups and medals. Sadly, Robert Harris passed away in Spring 2005.

'Your search is ended!' announced Thomas Criddle over the telephone a few days before the fifth CD in the *Better Land* series went for pressing. We had selected a record of Thomas singing Mendelssohn's *On wings of song* for inclusion but had, up to that point, little success in finding him. Denis Wright then suggested I use a new computer programme provided by British Telecom. Three Criddles were listed, so I wrote to the addresses given and two days later received the reply I had been hoping for but little expecting.

Thomas was born in Edmonton, London in March 1928. Like Derek Barsham, (but unknown to him) he had been a member of the Boys' Brigade in London until he was evacuated from the capital during the war. His singing career really began when, at the age of fourteen, he won first prize in a talent competition at the Granada Empire Cinema, Edmonton. The organist, Andrew Fenner happened to be playing, and two weeks later Sydney Bernstein, the manager of the Granada cinema chain, came to see Criddle's father with a view to engaging the boy to sing between the films. This was to be the start of his stage career and he appeared in many theatres. He earned on average £30 per performance for his concert and Vaudeville work and in 1943 he signed a contract with HMV and recorded several times at the Abbey Road Studios, always with his accompanist and manager Andrew Fenner

'I didn't need singing lessons by then,' he told me. 'We made many records but due to the war-time shortage of shellac only the more popular ones were released.' Thomas' recording of Bowler–Haydn Wood's, *I shall be there* and Linton–Young's, *I give thanks for you*, was made in January 1944 when he was almost sixteen and his voice had taken on a richer quality. 'I was told by several well-known lady sopranos that they wished they could hit the top notes with the same ease and accuracy that I could in those days!' Soon after that, he was filmed by British Pathé. In October 1943, Andrew Fenner Thomas wrote to Arthur Wynn at the BBC to tell him that Thomas, who was now fifteen, was 'reliable and widely-experienced' and suggested an audition. This was successful and Thomas was engaged to appear in the radio programme *Happidrome* in January the following year. More broadcasts followed and his fee was raised from five to eight guineas for an appearance with

Master Thomas Criddle

Albert Sandler and his orchestra in the 'Palm Court Hotel'.

After this, his manager felt that he should be given the chance of singing more serious music and asked for such engagements. However, the Music Department had lately discovered another boy soprano, Derek Barsham, whose style they preferred. But, unfortunately, they did not tell Mr Fenner that, and instead wrote that they thought the boy's voice was breaking and it would be wise not to plan future broadcasts. Mr Fenner was not happy about this and wrote personally to the Director General asking for an interview and telling him that 'the reasons given for the withholding of bookings do not satisfy me at all and are contrary to the truth.' As a result of this appeal, Thomas was given another audition in June, but this was not deemed satisfactory. Despite this rejection, Thomas was offered another broadcast later in the year. This was a success and he was engage to appear in several more programmes during the course of 1945.

'I was called up for National Service when I was eighteen but I was still giving concerts. Although my speaking voice had long since broken, my singing voice lasted until I was twenty-two. I even sang soprano at the training barracks and on occasions the sergeant would shout: "Criddle! Go home and fetch your records! I think my voice was eventually finished off by a combination of gin and cigarettes.'

Thomas Criddle became an actor and first broadcast in *Henry IV pt. 1* in January 1953. He has appeared on television and toured with many famous artistes, including Katherine Hepburn and Sir Donald Wolfit.

In England, the school leaving age was raised to fifteen in April 1947 and again to sixteen in 1972. Before the former date, boys could be, and often were, working on the stage and in full time employment from the end of the term in which they had reached fourteen. These and other changes in employment law (coupled with the demise of Music Hall itself) brought to an end the long and fascinating tradition of which the boys featured in this chapter were part. Happily, through recordings and personal reminiscences, we can still glimpse something of this vanished world.

The Broadcast Boys

Thetford Boys' Council School Choir, 1937
Robert Regent is seated at the extreme right of the middle row

The names of some of the boys engaged to sing on the radio are well-known due to the fact that they also made commercial records. However it is uncertain just how many boys sang in broadcasts, as few BBC recordings survive. Although it was the practice during the last war to re-use discs after washing them in acid, many recordings did survive until more recent times when the BBC destroyed countless recordings, claiming that they did not have sufficient storage space. If these discs had been written historical documents, their destruction would have been considered wanton vandalism.

Most of the boys featured in this book appeared in the hugely popular *Children's Hour*, which began in 1922, first on The National Programme and then in the Home Service. With regional variations, it was one of the largest departments of the BBC and many artistes began their broadcasting careers on this programme. For Denis Wright, Derek Barsham and Billy Neely, it opened up opportunities to broadcast in other BBC programmes. It is not known how many boys had been auditioned by the Director of *Children's Hour*, Derek McCulloch, and his assistant, May Jenkin.

Amongst the 'lost' voices chosen to appear in the mid-forties were those of Eric Theaker who, like Denis Wright, was trained by Harry Smith and also sang with the Kentucky Minstrels; and also Trevor Ling, a young boy soprano from Norwich. It was the policy of the BBC not to audition artistes under the age of twelve but an exception was made for eleven-year-old Trevor who was heard in January 1945. May Jenkin reported that he had 'an attractive little voice but needed to improve his breath control.'

Trevor's father persisted with the boy's training and he was invited to broadcast in April of that year, singing a selection of songs including *Where my caravan has rested* by Hermann – Löhr. He was to appear twice more, in October and in April 1946, when, after the latter broadcast, his voice was judged by the BBC to be 'much improved'. He was then invited to take part in the prestigious BBC programme *On Wings of Song*, with George Thalben-Ball as accompanist.

Unfortunately, Trevor was singing in the same period as Derek Barsham, who was three years older and much more experienced. However Dr. Leslie Ridge, Derek Barsham's manager, heard Trevor's broadcast and wrote to the BBC suggesting that Trevor, Eric Theaker and Derek sing together, with Dr. Thalben-Ball as accompanist. However, this could not be arranged and, sadly, Trevor's voice did not last long after that, breaking in 1947 when he was thirteen. He later studied at the Royal School of Music and has recently retired as a bass lay-clerk of Westminster Cathedral Choir.

Perhaps one of the most moving performances featured in *The Better Land* CD series, is Robert Regent's, recorded in January 1938. As result of our appeal in *Evergreen* magazine, Peter Regent contacted me and offered to lend two privately-recorded discs which he had kept in the hope that one day they would be published. His brother, Robert, had been killed in 1943, at the age of nineteen, whilst serving as a wireless operator on an RAF Air-Sea Rescue launch, which had been attacked by enemy aircraft, set on fire, and sunk.

Born in 1924 in Suffolk, Robert grew up in Thetford, Norfolk, where he sang with local church choirs and the *Thetford Boys' Council School Choir*, under the direction of Mr James Lee, a formidable headmaster and enthusiastic musician. The school's senior and junior choirs regularly carried-off all the banners for which they competed at the annual choral festival in Norwich, and Mr Lee also galvanised the local population into rehearsing and performing Gilbert & Sullivan operas and various pantomimes with Robert singing some of the leading rôles. The school choir broadcast on the BBC *Children's Hour* in 1937 and 1938, with Robert as soloist, and it was during this time that the two songs chosen for *The Better Land Volumes 4* and *5* were recorded.

Following our appeal on BBC Radio Norfolk, Jill Staplehurst was able to put us in touch with Robert's accompanist, Freda Taylor, who is now in her nineties. During a live radio interview Miss Taylor was able to give details of Robert's singing career and of his broadcasts with the choir to which he belonged. In 1964, the BBC ended *Children's Hour* despite strong protest from the many listeners and these concerned that quality programmes should continue to be made for children. However, the world was changing fast and, despite the matter being raised in Parliament, the programme was discontinued. Uncle Mac had already left some time before, but David Davies (Uncle David) continued until the end, closing the final edition with a reading of Oscar Wilde's *The Selfish Giant*. 'Tea, toast and Children's Hour' was no more and, sadly, even the recording of that final programme has been destroyed – just a short extract remaining in the archives.

The Temple Church Boys

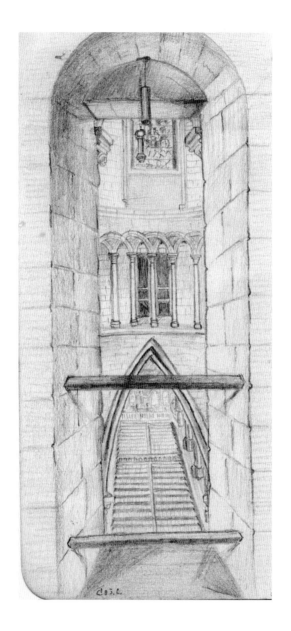

From the Triforium, Temple Church
drawing by C.O.J. Cocking, who died in the Great War

The choir of the Temple Church, London holds a special – almost revered - place in our story. No other choir was so universally well-known during the period covered in this book. Ernest Lough's recording of Mendelssohn's *Hear my prayer* immediately shot to fame when it was released in 1927. The history of the church and its choir has been well-documented by my friend and colleague David Lewer, who became a member in 1931 and, while still in his teens, wrote an account, which eventually was published in 1961 under the title *A Spiritual Song*.

It is mainly thanks to David that we are able to tell the story of the soloists of the choir. He has also helped prepare this chapter and has freely given permission to quote from his earlier writings and his new autobiography, *Just in Time*.

The Temple Church is one of London's greatest treasures. It lies in the west of the City and belongs to the two major Inns of Court, the Inner and Middle Temple. The church was built by the crusading Order of Knights Templar, founded to protect pilgrims on the road to the Holy City. The Round Church, in transitional Romanesque style, followed the plan of the Church of the Holy Sepulchre and was consecrated in honour of the Blessed Virgin Mary in 1185 by Heraclius, Patriarch of Jerusalem. The Quire, in 'heavenward-aspiring Gothic', was consecrated on Ascension Day, 1240, in the presence of Henry III and his court.

Following the dissolution of the Order of Knights Templar at the beginning of the 14th century, lawyers settled into the Temple, forming themselves into the Honourable Societies of the Inner and Middle Temple, two of the four Inns of Court. The governing body of Benchers acquired the freehold of the precinct from James I in 1608, one of the conditions being that they were to maintain the Temple Church and its services for ever, and this it has been their pride to do through four centuries. The church remains a Royal Peculiar, the private chapel of these two Inns of Court, and is not subject to Episcopal jurisdiction.

The modern choir was created following a major restoration of the church in 1842, when the Benchers decided that a cathedral-type service should be introduced. That there was a Temple Church Choir in the times of the Knights Templar, is clear from an item, '28 choir copes and four little copes for the Choristers', found in an Inventory of the contents of the Church in 1308 at the suppression of the Order in England. The choir did not survive the upheavals of the Reformation but was re-established for the re-opening of the church.

Under Dr. E.J.Hopkins, Organist from 1843 to 1898, the Temple Choir became famous and was the model for hundreds of surpliced choirs which sprang up in the Metropolis and beyond during the latter half of the 19th century.

When Dr Henry Walford Davies succeeded Dr Hopkins in 1898, he broadened the musical repertory, introducing in paticular the monthly cantata services which included the annual performances of

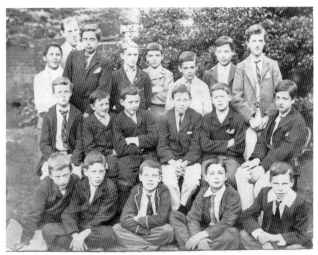

The Temple Choir, circa 1905.
Behind- Dr. Walford Davies. *Back* - R. Stansfeld, G. Layton, R. Perdue, L. Hall, H. Lee, D.E.M. Hay. *Middle* - L. Heyes, A.R. Waddams, C. Cocking, P. Walford, M. Capener, A.C. Dixon. *Front* - F. Steele, H.W. Capener, W. Irons, N. Stone, L. Adams.

Bach's *St. Matthew Passion* and the *Christmas Oratorio* followed by the Carols in the Round. George Thalben-Ball, who succeeded Walford Davies in 1919, maintained and enhanced the great musical traditions of the Temple and is regarded by many as the greatest choirmaster in living memory.

In May 1941, the Temple Church was grievously burnt-out during the last and worst night of the Blitz. Although much of the fabric survived, the organ containing 'Father' Smith's original pipework was destroyed. Also lost was all the music and some of the documents, though, thankfully, others had already been removed from the church by David Lewer and have been preserved.

Dr Hopkins had established a reputation for the training of soloists and there have undoubtedly been many since 1842. Sadly we have no means of hearing and judging these lost voices although photographs of several choristers remain.

John Calvert was the first choirmaster in 1842 before Hopkins was appointed in 1843. He engaged the original six boys to sing with the three professional men, and soon added two boys and three men to establish a perma-nent choir of four-

The Practice Room, Temple Church, 1941

teen voices. The two principal boys were paid £15 per annum and the four juniors £10 each.

William Hayman Cummings (1831-1915) was eleven years old when he joined the Temple Choir after having been a chorister at St Paul's, where he had sung at the funeral of Thomas Attwood in March 1838. He conducted a Temple Choral Club which con-sisted of those of his fellow choristers who were 'play-ers upon instruments.' As an alto, he sang in 1847 in a performance of Mendelssohn's *Elijah* at the Exeter Hall, conducted by the composer, who asked his name and wrote it upon his own visiting card, giving it to the singer. Cummings became organist of WalthamAbbey at the age of sixteen and returned to the Temple Church to sing tenor from 1853-59. In

The Temple Church, pre-1914 drawing by C.O.J. Cocking

1896 he was appointed Principal of the Guildhall School of Music.

On 11th June 1843, many of the nobility attended morning service at the Temple where Jeremiah Clarke's anthem *How long wilt Thou forget me, O Lord?* was sung; the treble solo by John Lloyd. Lloyd later sang cantoris bass at Temple (1852-68).

Not many of the names of the early boy choristers are known, until we come to a book of 'Agreements of Entry' kept by Hopkins from 1870, but some can be traced from other sources. Aynsley Cook (b.1835) the grandfather of Eugene Goossens, must have joined the choir soon after Hopkins arrived as choirmaster. Hopkins thought the boy of ten good enough to give him the solo soprano position. At eleven, Cook sang solos at the opening of St. George's RC Cathedral, Southwark, and a year later became 'Chamber Singer' to the Marquis of Anglesea. Later, he had a fine bass voice and sang for many years with the Carl Rosa Company. He declared his repertory to include 92 operas!

At the funeral of the Duke of Wellington in St. Paul's in 1852, the choirs of St Paul's Cathedral, Westminster Abbey, the Chapel Royal and the Temple took part. There was a persistent legend that a boy sang solo over the open 'grave', and that he was Henry Sanders, '1st Chorister of the Temple'.

George Ansell was singing in the choir between 1856 and 1863. He was probably Head Boy in 1861 and sang at the memorial service for the Prince Consort. At the last minute, Hopkins decided to change the anthem and chose one containing a difficult solo. The organist Sir John Goss happened to be in the congregation and after the service congratulated Hopkins on the rendering of the anthem. He asked him how long they had been practising it, and on

A Spiritual Song

hearing that it was rehearsed only that morning Goss asked to speak to the Head Boy, who was produced and was thereupon tipped a golden sovereign.

A hitherto unknown soloist's name has come to light through the researches made by the Revd Stephen Keeble who has kindly given us a copy of a memorial of the Revd George Rothwell. Mr Keeble has written an account of the work of George's brother, who rebuilt the organ for Walford Davies in 1910.

George Rothwell was born in 1855 in Liverpool and sang for four years in the parish church of Middleton. In 1867 the family moved to London and soon after he became a chorister at the Temple Church where he quickly attracted considerable attention by his beautiful voice. His brother Frederick wrote: 'What used to distinguish him most from the very first was [the] absence of boyish nervousness when singing or playing: the confident manner in which he would tackle difficult solos at the Temple ... often gained him great praise. I remember on one occasion after he had sung a solo ... a complete stranger met him as he was leaving the church and insisted [on] giving him a sovereign.' George Rothwell was received into the Roman Catholic Church in 1873 but, sadly, he died in 1882 in his 27th year.

Walter Lewis was Head Boy and soloist in 1882; his brother Ernest followed similarly in 1888. About this time six Temple choristers sang at several concerts for the composer Otto Goldschmidt at the Albert Hall. His wife, the celebrated soprano Jenny Lind, would come to the Temple practice-room to run through their parts with them, always bringing packets of sweets in sugar-loaf bags. She was then in her sixties and last sang in public in 1883.

We now come to the celebrated Henry Joseph Humm. He was accepted as a 'supernumerary' at the age of eight in 1881 and continued to sing until 1890. His voice was legendary: all who heard him were unanimous in the opinion that his singing was exceptionally mature, even, and expressive.' A.E. Wildey, a new chorister in 1889, first heard him sing *O for the wings of a dove*. 'I was spell-bound. I had never heard a voice like it, or since. I consider Joe Humm the most perfect boy singer I ever heard, and that he just 'pipped' Lough.' Ernest Minnion wrote: 'I can remember Joey as a marvellous solo boy, and to this day I do not believe I have ever heard his superior. Two indelible impressions remain in my mind - Joey's *Hear my prayer* and his solo in Mozart's *Glory, Honour, Praise and Power*. The treble solo makes a tremendous demand on the singer.'

In celebration of Queen Victoria's Golden Jubilee in 1887, a masque was held at the Inner Temple before Princess Louise. A report in *The Daily Telegraph* said: 'The voices of the Temple Church Choir gave sweet expression to the madrigals ... but it was a boy, and rather a little boy, named Henry Humm, who made the greatest hit in the evening's vocalization, singing the song *Orpheus with his lute* to the music of Arthur Sullivan. A rapturous encore brought the youngster back to the stage.'

Alfred Capel Dixon was a chorister from 1900 to 1907, and then sang as a tenor until his sudden death in 1949. He was one of the first new choristers with Walford Davies, and wrote of Doctor Davies' fascinating eloquence and his choir-training. 'Long before Master Lough's time there was a succession of boy soloists trained by 'Doctor', who testified to his power of inspiring a singer with the right technique without spoiling his natural gifts. One Sunday afternoon there were eight solos for different boys, all of whom were competent and showed good form.'

Alfred Capel Dixon

One of these was Charles 'Chink' Cocking (1901-07). He had a voice of beautiful quality and was cantoris-soloist for over three years, retaining his voice until the age of seventeen. Sadly he was killed in France.

But, to all at Temple, Dixon was the best singer and musician and most beloved of all. C.T. Waddams wrote: 'I have treasured memories of Dixon singing *I know that my Redeemer liveth* and decades later of his tenor solos. He was the greatest chorister both as man and boy that I have ever known.'

E.S. Ripley (1907-11) believed that the choir was at its best during his time as Head Boy and soloist. In 1909 'Pip' Ripley sang the difficult solo *Ye now are sorrowful* from Brahms' *Requiem* on 'Cantata Sunday', which was the third in each month. At a wedding in April 1911 at Christ Church, Lancaster Gate, he sang the solo *Love one another* and, apart from the normal fee, he was given - guess what - a beautiful golden sovereign. At last, and nearly eighteen, he left the choir. A total stranger, George Bentall, wrote 'to express great appreciation of your admirable work as "Leading Boy". I feel sure, from what I have seen of the kindly feelings existing between Dr. Walford Davies and the boys of the choir, that the years spent at the Temple must have proved happy indeed, but, believe me, such happiness is only a tithe of that which you have given … to the many who have no means of showing their gratitude.'

But there were still more singers to follow. Louis Bothamley, the Head Boy in 1914, had a voice of rare quality and as a soloist became a worthy successor to Ripley. Albert Buckley (1911-18) became head boy and soloist and a great leader with a fine team. During the war the choir sang at many camp concerts for the troops where 'Buckles' repeated his famous *You'll get there* (Parry).

Towards the end of the war, *Messiah Part III* was sung at Temple: Doctor Davies wrote in the old choristers' magazine, *The Templar,* that 'Buckles sang *I know that my Redeemer liveth* as well as I have ever heard it sung.' On his first visit to Temple, George Thalben-Ball heard Buckley singing and said that he had never heard such a beautiful voice.

We now approach the period covered by *The Better Land* series of CDs. The first two attempts at recording the choir had been in December 1922 and

February 1924, under Walford Davies and assisted by Mr Ball. These discs were not issued, however, and the first soloist to be recorded, Ernest Lough, was born in November 1911. Recently credited as 'the most famous choirboy in the world' he undoubtedly inspired many to seek a choristership after hearing his voice. To a great extent, Ernest Lough was in the right place at the right time, and his recording of Mendelssohn's *Hear my prayer* made for him a place in history.

Master Ernest Lough

Ernest Arthur Lough began his singing career as a chorister at St Peter's, Forest Gate and, following an unsuccessful audition for the choir of Southwark Cathedral, was interviewed at the Temple Church in 1924. 'I remember [at my audition] having to read an extract from a murder trial in *The News of the World*. Mr Ball accepted me with a warning: "You're getting a bit old," he said. "You had better hurry up". I was only twelve years old at the time!'

Lough - 'Fluff' to his fellows - became a pupil at the City of London School where since 1897 the Temple choristers have been educated. Every day except Wednesday the boys would leave school at 3.30p.m. to rehearse at Temple. After practice on Sundays there was normally half an hour before the service, so they would go down to the Temple gardens to run around before Matins. Lough always believed that this 'run-around' actually helped their singing. 'We would return to the church exhausted with sweat running all over our collars. Maybe it was some kind of treatment?'

By 1927, Lough was one of the soloists in the choir which was then blessed with exceptional voices, including those of Douglas Horton and Ronald Mallett. Microphone recording had just been introduced and HMV had invested in a mobile recording unit. In April of that year the choir assembled in church and Lough was perched on two large bibles in order to be nearer to the single microphone. Due to outside interruptions, Mendelssohn's *Hear my prayer* had to be recorded several times before the engineers were satisfied with the results.

Ernest Lough, Douglas Horton, and Ronald Mallett

This disc was issued a few weeks later and the sales figures took everyone by surprise - it was HMV's biggest seller for 1927. Six presses had to be set aside at the Hayes factory for its production. Later it was to sell a million copies and in 1962 Dr Ball and Ernest Lough were each presented with a golden disc to mark the occasion – although by this time HMV had lost count of the number of discs sold!

The recording master quickly wore out and a second was made in March 1928, by which time Lough was sixteen and his voice had taken on a fuller, richer tone. Lough always preferred the original record, describing his voice as 'crisper', but it is the second recording which is the most widely available. In August 1927, Lough and fellow-chorister Ron Mallett had recorded *I waited for the Lord* from Mendelssohn's *Hymn of Praise*, and it was soon after that Mr Ball told HMV there were definite signs of Lough's voice breaking.

The boy's voice was, in fact, to last another sixteen months, during which time he made some of his best discs, including Schubert's *Who is Sylvia?* in June 1928. Ernest Lough remained in the choir until 1929. He then went to work at HMV and served in the Auxiliary Fire Service during the war. When the choir was re-established he was, like several of the pre-war boys, to return as a 'Gentleman' and remained until the retirement of Dr. Ball in 1981.

Ronald Mallett was the younger brother of Jack Mallett, who had been Head Boy in 1924, and was related to the celebrated Henry Humm. Sadly, and cruelly, Ron lost his young life in a Japanese prisoner of war camp in 1945.

Harold Langston was born in 1916 and brought up in Whitley Bay, Northumberland. Early in 1929 he was 'discovered' at a music festival and, as Mr Ball (or 'Pill', as he was affectionately known before the war) was searching for experienced choristers to replace Lough, Horton, Mallett, and Jack Salisbury, he persuaded Mrs Langston to send Harold to the Temple, where he lodged with fellow choristers. The principal soloists of the choir at this time were the Head Boy, 'Tim' Leibe and Denis Barthel who followed him. Barthel made his first record, Sterndale

Bennett's *Remember now thy creator* in 1930 as a duet with Langston, but it was never released. David Lewer adds that 'Langston had a voice of almost perfect quality' and it is inexplicable that the two other songs recorded by Langston were not released until featured in the sister series of *The Better Land*, *The Glory of the Temple Church Choir*.

Master Harold Langston

Langston left the choir in 1932, returning briefly to sing tenor at the outbreak of the war before registering as a conscientious objector. He then took up farming, which was a reserved occupation, and emigrated to Canada in 1951. He died there in 2002.

Masters Langston, Berry, and Ratcliffe, circa 1930

Denis Barthel was born in May 1916. He commenced his career as a chorister at St Stephen's Church, Westminster, under its organist and choirmaster Dr William Bunney. When Denis was eleven he was taken by Bunney to the Temple for an audition by George Thalben-Ball. 'I shall never forget how kind he was at

Master Denis Barthel

my audition, and the encouragement he gave to a terrified young boy. I became a probationer in November 1927 when Lough was much involved in recording. Ernest was very kind and helped me enormously during my early days at Temple.'

Denis had made his debut as a soloist early the following year at the concert in the Middle Temple Hall singing Parry's *Ripple on*, but his most memorable performance was on Armistice Day 1931, when he sang solo the much-loved setting by the Revd C Harris of Sir John Arkwright's hymn *O Valiant Hearts* before King George V and Queen Mary and a packed audience in the Royal Albert Hall. This was the first world broadcast of the Festival of Remembrance, an awe-inspiring experience.

'The hall was very dimly lit; poppy petals were falling from the ceiling, and I was positioned adjacent to the organ loft high up in the hall from where I was looking out through a dim light at a mass of humanity. It really was quite frightening. I was accompanied in the later verses of the hymn by George Dixon and Frank Hastwell, both Gentlemen of the choir and mentors of mine.' Denis became principal soloist after Lough left the choir and Head Boy after Tim Leibe's voice broke in 1932, at a salary of three guineas a quarter. It was during this period that he made several of his records, the most enduring being Parry's *Jerusalem*, with pre-war sales amounting to half a million copies. But it was his rendition of *He was despised* from *Messiah* that impressed the critics when it was released in *The Better Land* series in 1999. 'For my solos I stood in the front row of the choir stalls on Cantoris side, lighted by a single lamp; Mr. Ball played from the organ loft, which was also lit but otherwise the church was in complete darkness and totally silent. It was a strange and emotional experience. I sang into a single microphone positioned immediately in front of me which also picked up the sound of the organ. In the recordings I made with the choir, the ensemble was not conducted: "Pill" played from the organ loft, and it was the task of the head boy on Decani side to lead. This responsibility developed fine qualities in the boys, and was a wonderful preparation for the future.'

'I sang in the choir until July 1933 when, after a practice, Mr Ball said "I think you had better come down from the stalls and sit with the probationers." I knew then that my time was coming to an end. I was sad to leave Temple and left with a heavy heart'. After working for an insurance company in the city, he embarked on what was to become a distinguished military career and retired

Major Denis Barthel and Stephen R. Beet

with the rank of Major.

In 1969, he and his family emigrated to Vancouver where he founded a successful marine equipment distributorship. In 2005, Denis Barthel still heads the company as Chairman of the Board. Major Barthel was twice mentioned in despatches and, like his father before him, was awarded the MBE.

It was during Denis Barthel's time as head boy that David Lewer became a chorister and, through his efforts, the life and times of the choir became well documented. In February 1931, David had been turned down as too old by Stanley Roper at the Chapel Royal, but it was suggested he try the Temple. 'Mr Ball greeted me with the greatest kindness and encouragement, asking me to sing various notes given at the piano. "How high could I sing?" I reached A adequately. "Did I play the piano?" Yes, a little. "Did I know the Psalms? No? But you can learn them."

'After singing my prepared song, I was asked the colour of Farmer Brown's grey horse and told to come along on Friday for the practice after school. I didn't know I was accepted as a chorister until a week or so later when "Pill" came up to me asking why I had not been at the Sunday service. "I hadn't been told to come," I said. "Oh , but you must!" he exclaimed, "I want you."' This was to be the beginning of a lifetime's devotion to the choir. 'I was immediately entranced, and even more so when I heard for the first time the boys singing, on their own, Elgar's *Doubt not thy Father's care*. Could I sing like that?

Well, I could as soon as I had been taught by such a genius. How quickly we learnt as we instinctively knew that he was the best ever choirmaster! We loved him, and wanted to be the finest choir in England.' David's brief period of glory came when

Mr Ball thought that his voice would successfully match that of Jack Phillips very well. They sang a number of duets, Jack taking the upper part, until in 1933 David's voice broke.

'Mr Ball found it difficult to tell a boy he could no longer be in the choir – or to "turn the cracks out" - and he suggested that I rest my voice. But he put me in charge of the music (or 'books', as it was called), and I would sometimes turn pages for him at the organ. It was during those years that I was able to begin my research into the history of the choir'.

A prominent soloist in the mid-thirties was Thomas Meddings,, who was born in Walthamstow in 1922. When he was ten he was auditioned by GTB and became a probationer in 1932. Ernest Lough was by then a smart young man a few years out of the choir and was seen only occasionally as a fleeting presence in the organ loft. 'That caused a buzz among the boys,' Tom adds. 'What did he think of us? Were we up to standard?'

'From the probationers' mid-church stall I pieced together as best I could what the work of the choir was about, and in due time became a full chorister, singing on Decani side. Before long, a few beginners' solos came my way, and in due course I sang most of the

Master Thomas Meddings, 1937

traditional treble solo repertoire. My favourite was the *Benedictus* from Mozart's *Requiem*, but the supreme musical experience was a choral one - the *Gratias Agimus Tibi* from Bach's Mass in B minor.'

'Dr. Ball's practices were always enjoyable. He was never stuffy, effortlessly commanding total attention; and he taught as much by example as by precept, using his own fine voice to illustrate points.' Denis Barthel adds that 'we were taught to project our voices forward into the head and not through the nose, thus avoiding the so-called 'cathedral hoot'. In short, we were taught a head tone. As a result, a number of our boys sang until they were seventeen.'

Tom took part in a schools' radio programme with the conductor Ernest Read, who had asked for *I know that my Redeemer liveth* to be prepared. 'I rehearsed this with Dr Ball and then with Mr Read on the morning of the broadcast which was to take place in the afternoon. Returning to Broadcasting House after lunch, I found that Read had changed his mind and, recruiting a trumpeter, now wished to substitute *Let the Bright Seraphim*, which I had never sung. After a cursory run-through, the broadcast proceeded smoothly with brass obbligato, much to the surpriseof Dr Ball who heard the transmission elsewhere.'

Masters T. Meddings and
D. Horgan

'The choir with Meddings as Head Boy is promising,' David Lewer wrote at the time; so it proved to be, and it is surprising that no records were made during this period. Meddings had recorded

Spohr's *Lord God of Heaven and Earth in* 1933 as a duet with Dennys Lake and he remembers that Lake's rich contralto voice on the record was unmistakable. 'When the disc was published, he invited me to spend a Saturday at his home in Hampstead to celebrate, at one point transmitting the recording to a friend via the telephone.'

Lake was, by this time, an experienced soloist and at the Aldershot Tattoo of 1934, tens of thousands had heard his recording of a verse of *Abide with me*. At the Coronation of King George VI and Queen Elizabeth, Tom was one of the 'First Twelve' Temple boys to sing at Westminster Abbey but, the following spring, when he was sixteen, he had to leave the choir.

'Like all trebles, it was frustrating to be deprived of my voice just as my musical understanding was growing and I recall a *Hear Ye, Israel* just before the end which satisfied me more than anything I had done.'

After war service, including a tour of duty in Burma and French Indo-China, Tom Meddings studied architecture and, as a senior architect with the Corporation of the City of London, was responsible for the design of the new City of London School. He died just before Christmas 2004, a few weeks after approving the draft of this chapter.

In November 1935 George Thalben-Ball had been awarded the Lambeth degree of Doctor of Music. But Walford Davies was still revered at Temple and made occasional visits, so GTB did not assume the title of 'Doctor' until Walford's death in 1941.

In 1938 Allan Young and Kenneth Kedge were becoming first-rate soloists and duettists. Kedge sang Wesley's *Love one another* at a wedding for which he was given a silver spoon. David Lewer wrote, 'I shall never forget Kedge's singing, with Tom Budgett (bass), in Michael Wise's *The ways of Zion remain*. Alan Polgrean's *Benedictus* (Mozart) was fine too' Undoubtedly their singing would have been recorded but unfortunately the war prevented this. At the outbreak of hostilities, the boys were sent for safety to Marlborough College. Back in London it was decided to keep the church open as long as possible despite the onslaught of the Blitz.

The gentlemen of the choir had been joined by other ex-choristers including, for a time, David Lewer and Harold Langston, and services continued, the choir on occasion singing to the congregation assembled in the basement shelter during air raids. The boys returned several times during the holidays and there was even talk of admitting new boys to prolong the life of the choir but, sadly, this was not to be.

Temple Church and Inner Temple Hall, circa 1945

The Temple was probably the only central London church with a full choir of boys at that time and on Easter Day 1941 - when ten boys and twelve men were present at Morning Service - the anthem was Beethoven's *Hallelujah* from *Christ at the Mount of Olives*. But this was destined to be the last time the boys would sing in the old Temple Church.

Immediately after the bombing in May 1941, ex-choristers and friends decided to hold a short informal weekly service in the ruins throughout the war. This they did until l954, when, following the most careful restoration, the Quire was rededicated by the Archbishop of Canterbury in the presence of Queen Elizabeth the Queen Mother. For that happy day in March the chorister boys were loaned by Sir William McKie, Organist of Westminster Abbey. In the following year, the choir was re-established, the first Head Boy being Robin Fairhurst who, at the age of fourteen, was a singer of considerable experience.

He was born in London in 1941 and at the age of eleven won a Junior Scholarship to Trinity College of Music, London, where he studied piano, violin, harmony and composition. He sang in several BBC broadcasts, including the 'Welcome-Back' concert at the London Palladium for the newly crowned Queen after her world-tour of the Commonwealth in 1954. A photo of his father's painting of him as a choirboy appeared in Radio Times that week.

That same year, Decca engaged him for two solo records to be made in the Kingsway Hall with Charles Smart at the organ: the first was *The Lord's my shepherd* to the tune *Crimond,* one of the last 78s pressed, and the second a 45rpm record of Bach's *Sheep may safely graze* and Handel's *Where e'er you walk*. He also regularly appeared as Robin in the BBC pro-gramme 'Chapel in the Valley' with Sandy

'Portrait of Robin"
Mr. J. Fairhurst at work on the portrait of his son.

McPherson.

At the Temple, he met the tenor George Dixon, who was Head of Schools' Broadcasting and able to obtain acting rôles for him. He also sang with Benjamin Britten and the English Opera Group and was selected to understudy David Hemmings in *The Turn of the Screw*, as already mentioned in an earlier chapter. Robin later featured in recordings of Britten cantatas, such as *Rejoice in the Lamb*.

When his voice broke at the age of sixteen, Robin won a singing scholarship to Trinity College of Music, London from where his career blossomed. Several Templars saw him in Malcolm Williamson's opera *Our Man in Havana*. In 1975 Robin Fairhurst became Head of the Vocal Department at the Folkwang School of Music in Essen, from which position he retired in 2004.

By the late 1950s the choir had reached the same high standard as that maintained by Dr

Thalben-Ball before the war. Another soloist from those days was Alan Bradbrook, who had been a chorister at the St. Mary of the Angels Choir School. George Dixon arranged for the boy to record his composition *The Beekeepers Introit*, as part of a BBC radio adaptation of William Mayne's *A Swarm in May*. HMV quickly renewed its interest in recording the choir, and several excellent discs were issued, the first in 1959.

Master Alan Bradbrook

But perhaps the best known soloists of the early 1960s are Robin Lough and Ian le Grice, who both sang in the first HMV LP to be issued in 1959. Robin, the second son of Ernest Lough, was, at the age of eight, the youngest member of the choir at the time of its re-formation, and Ian joined two years later in 1957. They also sang together in the recorded duet *The souls of the righteous* (Nares). Both possessed voices of rare quality and left the choir when they were over sixteen years old - Robin in 1962, and Ian a year later. Other prominent soloists were to follow and Michael James entered the choir as a very small boy in 1960 at the age of nine, and ceased singing at seventeen after two years as Head Boy. He can be heard as soloist in the hymn *Loving shepherd of thy sheep* on the 1967 HMV LP *Lift up your heads*. A talented musician, Michael became a music master at Canford School, then organist at Wimbourne Minster. He was about to take up a similar appointment at Rochester Cathedral when, sadly, he was struck down with cancer and died in

1981 at the age of thirty. Another fine soloist, Andrew Davies, joined the choir in 1967 and remained for four years. He sang *Pie Jesu* in Faure's *Requiem* memorably at a CLS rectal in the church in 1971.

Martin Griffiths recorded Handel's *He was despised* a week or two after its inclusion in a Sunday service in 1975, and this has been featured in *The Glory of the Temple Church Choir* CD series. In 1979, the BBC producer Paul Vaughan released on LP *Music from the Temple Church*, the soloists on that disc being David Abbott and Richard Matthews, joint Head Boys in 1977 when the record was made. Having heard of *Amphion's* intention to issue a definitive set of recordings of the choir, Paul Vaughan generously made available his master tapes, which form the basis of the third volume in the series.

Finally, Michael Ginn entered the choir in 1977 at the age of nine. He soon became a soloist and, in 1980, sang *Hear my prayer* in the *Abbey* recording of *The Temple Tradition.* Michael was in demand elsewhere as a singer and was noted for his performance as 'Miles' in Britten's *The Turn of the Screw* at the Colosseum.

After 62 years at the Temple Dr George Thalben-Ball retired in 1981 and was knighted in the following year. He died, aged 90, in 1987. Although officially 'Sir George', he will be for ever remembered affectionately as 'Doctor' by grateful generations of Temple Church choristers. We end our story here as, although other soloists were to follow, the departure of Sir George Thalben-Ball marked the end of an era that spanned a century or more. Walford Davies introduced suitable ex-choristers to the choir as 'Gentlemen', a tradition continued under Thalben-Ball. This enabled the formation of a better ensemble as all were trained by them as boys. A change came with the following choirmasters who introduced 'lay-clerks' as in cathedrals.

The unique 'Temple Tone', so evident on the *Amphion* recordings, and passed down from the days of Dr Hopkins and Walford Davies, quickly gave place to a more contemporary cathedral sound. But it is not for us to judge! Let us rejoice that for so long the Temple tradition had been in such expert hands and that so many recordings have been preserved. As David Lewer wrote, the story of this choir and its soloists is more than an historical account: it is indeed 'A Spiritual Song'.

Sir George Thalben-Ball

Just In Time

London Choir School, early 1920's

Master Walter Lawrence

Walter Lawrence was one of the first boy sopranos to commit his voice to wax. The US Columbia catalogue for 1915 announced that 'for the first time in the annals of the recording art, the perfect voice of a boy soprano has been adequately recorded - by the Columbia Gramophone Company. Approaching the celestial as nearly perhaps as anything mortal can, is the voice of Walter Lawrence, soloist of All Angels' Church, New York City. In its mingling of angelic purity and true musical beauty, the singing of this child passes the bounds of ordinary criticism and remains an example of tonal perfection and an auditory delight.'

Just as we were due to make the master disc of volume four of *The Better Land*, I was contacted by John Brookman who asked us to consider including his 1934 recordings of Adams' *The Star of Bethlehem* and *Nearer my God to thee*. Brookman joined the choir of St. Margaret's, Westminster in 1928. In those days the choirmaster, Stanley Roper, employed a professional boy soloist named John Griffith, who was a member of the London Choir School, already mentioned. But when Herbert Dawson took over the choir he encouraged the boys in the choir to take the solos, and Brookman and Eric Brown became the principal soloists, John remaining so for the remainder of his seven years in the choir. After Brown left, John was asked to record by HMV.

The record was made in the Kingsway Hall,

nine days before his sixteenth birthday, John choosing *The Star of Bethlehem* himself. The recording session lasted from two until five in the afternoon. 'The final take was the one used,' John remarked; 'and just before we finished the engineer played me one of the earlier waxes – it was the first time I had ever heard my voice and it was really spine chilling! By playing the wax in the van it was destroyed, so naturally I didn't hear the chosen recording until it was issued.'

One of the jobs of the head boy at St Margaret's (the church attended by Members of Parliament) was to come down from the stalls and hand a copy of the anthem personally to Mr. Speaker, who would follow the music diligently! John remained in the choir until 1935; after which Herbert Dawson found him a position in Barclay's Bank. For a leaving present, he had been given an inscribed watch, and Dawson remarked: 'In all your seven-and-a-half years, you have never missed a lead!' When in 1940 John returned badly injured from the beaches of Dunkirk, the watch was still going, and it kept faithful time until the day he died, in December 2003

During the evacuation of the City of London School to Marlborough College in 1939, a story was put about that a Temple chorister had sang a particularly effective rendition of Mendelssohn's *Hear my prayer* in the college chapel and the boy's name was Brian Moody. This in fact was not the case and we were able to trace Brian to Perth, Western Australia where he explained that he had indeed been a CLS schoolboy but not a member of the Temple Church Choir. His voice was recorded but the discs were not issued until two were featured in *The Better Land* series.

In 1948 eight-year-old Beverley Jones became a

chorister at York Minster under the young Francis Jackson and was to become one Dr. Jackson's finest soloists. Bev represented the Minster at the Coronation of The Queen in June 1953, and became Head Boy the following year. One of the song men (as the gentlemen of the choir are called), John Rothera was in the habit of regularly recording the sung services (hanging a single microphone aloft between the choir stalls before it was removed by order of the Dean and Chapter!). In 1954 he recorded Bev's performance of *A Song of Peace* and other works by Stanford and these recordings were later featured in *The Better Land* series.

Thomas Tweedie of Tyneside, and Trevor Schofield, both feature briefly in our series and their story remains to be written; likewise we have made no attempt to detail the lives of Dennis Diehl, Trevor Middleton, Bobby Breen, James Phelan, and Teddy Jones, all of whom were recorded soloists but have not yet appeared in the series.

Master Trevor Schofield

Michael Morley features significantly but, sadly, we are able to relate nothing of his life! It is surprising that it has so far been impossible to trace him. He recorded for Decca in the early 1950s, and was one of the first artistes to be heard on 33rpm.

The number of boys who made recordings before the Second World War is unknown but is certainly over one hundred in total. Our story has featured perhaps the best and most famous, but who knows what further discoveries remain to be made?

Afterword

We have, in this book, undertaken much more than a 'musical journey from boyhood to manhood' (as Derek Barsham described his life) – more even than a social history. It is the story of events which at one time or another touched the lives of many people throughout the last century. Only those born before 1930 remember how different the world was before the Second World War. Those who do remember, find it extremely difficult to convey the pre-war standards and expectations. On the musical scene thousands of boys sang in hundreds of boys' choirs throughout the country, over one hundred church choirs of men and boys being reported in London alone in 1899! Boy sopranos were in great demand and schools like The London Choir School were set up to supply soloists for prestigious choirs and concerts.

The average chorister would expect to go on singing as a boy soprano well into his teens because the head tone and 'bel canto' methods taught in those days preserved the singing voice well beyond the natural break at puberty and resulted in the distinctive 'full-toned' sound, in those days regarded as a natural boy's voice, which some would now describe as 'feminine'. The harsher 'boy treble' sound so beloved of present day choirmasters was then almost unknown – or, if encountered, severely criticised.

After the war, Britain entered a new age and boy sopranos, like the *Children's Hour* radio programme which so often featured them, had no part in it. Children were encouraged to grow up before their time and during the 50s and 60s we lost our traditional respect for the learning of the past. Choirs and choirboys survived, of course, but not as we had known them: Dr. Francis Jackson has tellingly remarked that, during his final years as Organist of York Minster, he noticed a marked change of attitude. 'The boys did not "let themselves go" and produce the tone as they had in the past. It was almost as if they were embarrassed by their voices.'

In addition the old generation of skilled vocal teachers was passing away. Traditional Sunday Schools were sadly depleted and the ready supply of choirboys dried up except in cathedrals and those places lucky enough to have an inspiring and understanding choirmaster.

Many people listening to the recordings featured on *The Better Land* CD's, remark that the singers sound like trained women, thus indicating how much attitudes have changed in less than fifty years. The soloists were not, in fact, trained like women but like boys – which is why they were correctly referred to as 'boy sopranos', the term 'boy treble' not being used in popular terminology until the 1950s (although strictly correct as far as church choristers are concerned, I am informed!).

The end of childhood is an emotional experience, and recalling it sometimes sixty or more years after 'childish things have been put away' (to quote St. Paul), has often been difficult and traumatic for the boys featured in this book, especially when early success has led to heights of fame not achieved later in adult life. However, a whole generation or more later, each singer has been willing to relate his story to me, and I am aware of the privilege, and the responsibility, to tell these with sensitivity.

Many of the 'boys' have met for the first time and shared common experiences - several becoming personal friends as a result.

The journey to 'discover' these boy sopranos has taken me to many parts of the world and, if the story of *The Better Land* had not been told now, it might have been lost for ever.

Amphion Discography

[1]   **The Better Land** (Hemans-Cowen - special arrangement by Doris Arnold for Denis Wright)
Master Denis Wright With Doris Arnold's Kentucky Minstrels Conductor Leslie Woodgate Robinson Cleaver - organ. Rec. Grande Theatre, Llandudno July 1942 H.M.V. C.3313

[2]   **I Hear You Calling Me** (Harford-Marshall)
Master Leslie Day Rec. May 1933 Columbia D.B.1122

[3]   **He was Despised** (Handel) *Master Denis Barthel*
Rec. Temple Church, London Dr. George Thalben Ball - organ, 24th February 1932 H.M.V. B.4107

[4]   **Who is Sylvia?** (Schubert - arr. Geehl)
Master Robert Harris Acc. by Leslie Jeffries & Orchestra Rec. 17th June 1934   Parlophone E.7039-1

[5]   **O Lord Whose Mercies Numberless** (Handel)
Master Frederick Firth Rec. 10th March 1928 Test Pressing 8650107 Columbia Wax 3303-1

[6]   **Somewhere a Voice is Calling** (Newton & Tate)
Master John Bonner Rec. July 1930 Columbia D.B.136

[7]   **God Shall Wipe Away All Tears** (Sullivan)
Master Morris Steven With Stephani & his Silver Songsters Rec. 1936 Decca K.843

[8]   **O For the Wings of a Dove** (Mendelssohn)
Master Gordon Carter with the choir of Manchester Cathedral Rec. 1934 Rex. 8285

[9]   **Serenade** (Schubert)
Master Frederick Firth Rec. 10th March 1928 Columbia Test Pressing & Wax Columbia 3304

[10] **Smilin' Through** (Arthur A. Penn)
Master Derrick Jones Acc. by Scott Wood & Orchestra Rec. 25th May 1937 Regal Zonophone Test CAR 4562-1

[11] **Spring Morning** (Carey) *Master Walter Lawrence*
1914 acoustic recording Columbia 2517

[12] **If there were dreams to sell** (Ireland)
Master Frederick Firth Rec. September 1928, Test Pressing Brunswick Wax B.A. 347

[13] **Christopher Robin is saying his Prayers**
(A.A.Milne-H.Fraser Simson) *Master Denis Wright*
withDoris Arnold's Kentucky Minstrels Cond. Leslie
Woodgate Rec. as [1] H.M.V. C.3313
[14] **By an Old Abbey Door** (Towers, Leon, Nicholls)
Master Thomas Tweedie Rec. 1932 Decca F.3260
[15] **Goodnight Said the Cuckoo** (P.B. Harding)
Master Trevor Schofield Rec. 21st Dec. 1928 Columbia 5258
[16] **O Little Town of Bethlehem** (H. Walford Davies)
Master Denis Barthel Rec. Temple Church, London, Dr. G.
Thalben Ball - organ 24th February 1932 H.M.V. B.4285
[17] **The Last Rose of Summer** (Thomas Moore)
Master Denis Wright Gerald Moore - piano
Rec. 4th October 1941 H.M.V. B.9231
[18] **My Heart Ever Faithful** (Bach) *Master Frederick Firth*
Rec. 1928 Organist - Gerald Saxby Columbia 20074B
[19] **Nymphs & Shepherds** (Purcell)
Master John Bonner Rec. September 1929 Columbia 9840
[20] **Market Square** (Fraser Simson)
Master Denis Wright Acc. Gerald Moore Rec. 4th October
1941 Test Pressing H.M.V. OEA 9529
[21] **The Holy City** (Adams Weatherley) *Master Iwan
Davies* of the London Choir School
Rec. 1931 Decca K.632
[22] **For you alone** (P.J.O Reilly-Henry Geehl)
Master Leslie Day Rec. as [2] Columbia D.B. 1122

[1] **Jerusalem** (Parry-Blake) Master Denis Barthel
Rec. Temple Church, London, 24/2/32.
  Dr. George Thalben-Ball at the famous Father
Smith organ. H.M.V. B. 4258 [2.22]
[2] **Silent Worship** (Handel-Somervell) Master Derek
Barsham Phyllis Spurr - piano
    Rec. 1946 Decca F. 8913 [3.06]
[3] **Passing By** (E. Purcell-Herrick) Master Derek
Barsham Rec. as [2] [2.16]
[4] **Ninepenny Fiddle*** (Trad. arr. Moore) Master
Billy Neely, Gerald Moore-piano
  Rec. May 1950 Unpublished recording   [2.43]
[5] **Lark in the Clear air** (Trad-based on ancient air,
written by Sir Samuel Ferguson) *Master Billy Neely*
Rec. May 1950 H.M.V. C. 1850 [2.38]
[6] **Cradle Song** (Schubert-Claudius) Master Denis
Wright Gerald Moore-piano
    Rec. 4/10/41 H.M.V. B. 9231 [3.11]
[7] **I ll Walk Beside You** (Murry-Lockton)
Master Derek Barsham
String acc. cond. Phillip Green Rec. 1946 Decca M. 611
[3.03]
[8] **The Birds** (Britten-Belloc) *Master Billy Neely*
Gerald Moore-piano
    Rec. May 1950 H.M.V. 10041 [2.05]
[9] **Child and the Twilight*** (arr.Moore) Master Billy
Neely Gerald Moore-piano
    Rec. May 1950 Unpublished recording [2.25]
[10] **Remember now thy Creator*** (Sterndale-Bennett)
Masters Harold Langston &
    Denis Barthel with Temple Church Choir acc. Dr.
George Thalben-Ball. Rec. 3/7/30
    Unpublished recording [3.15]
[11] **Lullay Myn Lyking** (Trad. 15 Cent. arr. Terry)
Master Denis Barthel Temple Church Choir
    Dr. George Thalben-Ball piano acc. Rec.
2/2/32 H.M.V. B. 3976 [2.01]

[12] **Uncle Mac s Favourite Hymns, All Things Bright & Beautiful, There s a Friend for Little Children, Once in Royal David s City** Master Denis Wright with the Greenbank Children s Choir with Uncle Mac (Derek McCulloch) Frank A. Taylor-organ and Uncle David (Eric David Davis)-piano. Cond. Leslie Woodgate. Rec. 1941 H.M.V. B.D. 978/9 [4.30]

[13] **Hymn that I Sang as a Boy** (Miller-Burnaby) Master Graham Payn
Rec. 1934 Rex 8028a [3.20]

[14] **Meadowsweet*** (April) Master Graham Payn Rec. 1933
B.B.C. Transcription disc [1.52]

[15] **Anchor Song** (Smith) Master Derek Barsham Phyllis Spurr-piano
Rec. 1946 Decca M. 615 [2.50]

[16] **A Fairy Story by the Fire** (Merikanto) Master Billy Neely Gerald Moore-piano
Rec. 1950 H.M.V. B. 10150 [2.43]

[17] **Vergin Tutt Amor** (Francesco Durante) Master Billy Neely Gerald Moore-piano
Rec. 1950 H.M.V. B. 10096 [3.30]

[18] **Star of Bethlehem** (Adams-Weatherly) Master Derek Barsham Fela Sowande-organ
Rec. Kingsway Hall, May 1945 Decca K.1113 [4.48]

[19] **As pants the Hart** (Spohr) Master Thomas Meddings, Temple Church Choir,
Dr. George Thalben-Ball-organ Rec. October 1935 H.M.V. B. 838 0 [3.12]

[20] **Il Moi Bel Foco** (Benedetto Marcello-Baker) Master Billy Neely Gerald Moore-piano
Rec. 1950 H.M.V. B.10096 [3.29]

[21] **Nymphs & Shepherds*** (Purcell) Master Derek Barsham Nancy Phillips-violin
Children s Hour Broadcast B.B.C. Transcription disc 12 PD 21565 [3.37]

[22] **Cherry Ripe*** (Hurn-Herrick) Master Billy Neely Havelock-Nelson-piano

Children's Hour Broadcast 1949 B.B.C. Direct
Disc recording   [2.09]
[23] **Hallelujah** (Easter Hymn dating from 1623) Master
Denis Barthel acc. George Thalben-Ball
    at the famous Father Smith organ in the Temple
Church Rec. 1933 H.M.V. B. 4107   [2.33]
[24] **Star of God*** (Coates-Murray) Master Derek
Barsham Rec. live at the Royal Albert Hall
    (Boys Brigade Physical Phantasmagoria) March
1946 Direct Disc Recording   [3.20]
* Released for the first time ever

[1]   **The Better Land** (Hemans-Cowen - special arrangement by Doris Arnold for Denis Wright) Master Denis Wright With Doris Arnold's Kentucky Minstrels Conductor Leslie Woodgate Robinson Cleaver - organ Rec. Grande Theatre, Llandudno July 1942 H.M.V. C.3313

[2]   **I Hear You Calling Me** (Harford-Marshall) Master Leslie Day
     Rec. May 1933 Columbia D.B.1122

[3]   **He was Despised** (Handel) Master Denis Barthel Rec. Temple Church, London Dr. George Thalben- Ball - organ. 24th February 1932 H.M.V. B.4107

[4]   **Who is Sylvia?** (Schubert - arr. Geehl) Master Robert Harris Acc. by Leslie Jeffries & Orchestra Rec. 17th June 1934   Parlophone E.7039-1

[5]   **O Lord Whose Mercies Numberless** (Handel) Master Frederick Firth Rec. 10th March 1928 Test Pressing 865010 Columbia Wax 3303-1

[6]   **Somewhere a Voice is Calling** (Newton & Tate) Master John Bonner Rec. July 1930 Columbia D.B.136

[7]   **God Shall Wipe Away all Tears** (Sullivan) Master Morris Stevens With Stephani & his Silver Songsters Rec. 1936 Decca K.843

[8]   **O For the Wings of a Dove** (Mendelssohn) Master Gordon Carter With the choir of Manchester Cathedral Rec. 1934 Rex. 8285

[9]   **Serenade** (Schubert) Master Frederick Firth
     Rec. 10th March 1928
Columbia Test Pressing & Wax Columbia 3304

[10]   **Smilin Through** (Arthur A. Penn) Master Derrick Jones Acc. by Scott Wood & Orchestra Rec. 25th May 1937 Regal Zonophone Test CAR 4562-1

[11]   **Spring Morning** (Carey) Master Walter Lawrence
     1914 acoustic recording Columbia 2517

[12]   **If there were dreams to sell** (Ireland) Master Frederick Firth Rec. September 1928, Test Pressing Brunswick Wax B.A. 347

[13]   **Christopher Robin is saying his Prayers**

(A.A.Milne-H.Fraser Simson) Master Denis Wright with
Doris Arnold s Kentucky Minstrels
Cond. Leslie Woodgate Rec. as [1] H.M.V. C.3313
[14] **By an Old Abbey Door** (Towers, Leon, Nicholls)
Master Thomas Tweedie Rec. 1932 Decca F.3260
[15] **Goodnight Said the Cuckoo** (P.B. Harding)
    Master Trevor Schofield Rec. 21st December 1928
    Columbia 5258
[16] **O Little Town of Bethlehem** (H. Walford Davies)
    Master Denis Barthel Rec. Temple Church, London,
Dr. G. Thalben Ball - organ
24th February 1932 H.M.V. B.4285
[17] **The Last Rose of Summer** (Thomas Moore)   Master
Denis Wright Gerald Moore - piano
Rec. 4th October 1941 H.M.V. B.9231
[18] **My Heart Ever Faithful** (Bach) Master Frederick
Firth Rec. 1928 Organist - Gerald Saxby Columbia 20074B
[19] **Nymphs & Shepherds** (Purcell) Master John
Bonner Rec. September 1929 Columbia 9840
[20] Market Square (Fraser Simson) Master Denis
Wright Acc. Gerald Moore Rec. 4th October 1941
        Test Pressing H.M.V. OEA 9529
[21] **The Holy City** (Adams Weatherley) Master Iwan
Davies of the London Choir School
Rec. 1931 Decca K.632
[22] **For you alone** (P.J.O Reilly-Henry Geehl)
Master Leslie Day Rec. as [2] Columbia D.B. 1122

BETTER LAND 4   AMPHION PHI CD 168

[1] **Come Back** (Toselli s Serenade. Words R.H. Elkin) Master Leslie Day Rec.22/6/33. Columbia DB 1147 [2.52]

[2] **Abide with me** (Lyte-Liddle) Master John Bonner with orchestra. W.G. Webber, organ. Rec. Christ Church, Westminster Bridge Rd, London, Rec. 9/1/29. Columbia 9745 [4.02]

[3] **Five Eyes*** (Armstrong Gibbs) Master Billy Neely Havelock Nelson, piano. B.B.C. broadcast. Rec. 9/8/49. [1.05]

[4] **The Fairy Tree*** (Vincent O Brien) Master Billy Neely Havelock Nelson, piano. B.B.C. broadcast. Rec. 9/8/49. [2.10]

[5] **I will sing of Thy Great Mercies O Lord*** (Mendelssohn: St. Paul) Master Harold Langston George Thalben Ball, organ. Rec. Temple Church, 31/12/29. H.M.V. test BR 2713-2 [3.06]

[6] **Pierrot at the dance** (Lockton-Drummond) Master Trevor Schofield with piano. Rec. 9/5/29. Columbia 5528   [3.10]

[7] **One night of love** (Kahn-Schertzinger) Master Robert Harris acc. Leslie Jeffries & his orchestra at the Grand Hotel, Eastbourne. Rec. 1933. Parlophone R. 2102 [3.20]

[8] **Hark! Hark! the Lark*** (Schubert) Master Brian Moody Ernest Lush, piano. Rec. 26/5/44. Decca test pressing [2.32]

[9] **Slumber dear maid** (Handel) Master John Bonner with orchestra. Details as track [2] [3.25]

[10] **My heart ever faithful** (Bach) Master Raymond Kinsey with orchestra. Rec.24/4/33. H.M.V. C. 2571 [3.08]

[11] **The Old Church Bells*** (H.M.Farrar) Master Robert Harris acc. by Leslie Jeffries & orchestra. Parlophone test record, matrix CE. 6633-1 Rec. Grand Hotel, Eastbourne, 26/9/34. [3.17]

[12] **Love s old sweet song** (Bingham-Molloy) Master Robert Harris Details as track [7] [3.21]

[13] **The Trout*** (Schubert) Master Brian Moody

Ernest Lush, piano. Rec. 26/5/44. Decca test pressing [2.13]

[14] **Nursery Scene, Boris Godounov** (Moussorgsky) Master Derek Barsham with Gladys Palmer, London Symphony Orchestra. Cond. Stanford Robinson. Rec. 30/4/47. Matrix AR. 11093 issued as Decca K. 1601 [1.56]

[15] **Hear my prayer*** (Mendelssohn) Master Billy Neely with BBC Concert Choir & organ. Rec. Aeolian Hall, Kingsway, B.B.C. broadcast, November 1950. [4.00]

[16] **Star of Bethlehem** (Adams) Master John Brookman with Herbert Dawson, organ.
Rec. Kingsway Hall, 11/7/34. H.M.V. B. 8241 [3.26]

[17] **A Brown Bird Singing*** (Barrie-Haydn Wood) Master Robert Regent
Piano acc. Freda Taylor. Private recording 1938, matrix CP 517 [2.44]

[18] **I know that my Redeemer Liveth** (Handel) Master Ernest Lough George Thalben-Ball, organ. Temple Church. Rec.22/12/27. H.M.V. B. 2656   [6.31]

[19] **Hear ye, Israel*** (part1) (Mendelssohn) Master Ernest Lough with George Thalben-Ball, Temple Church, London. Unpublished H.M.V. test. Rec. August 1927. [2.59]

[20] **Kitty my love will ya marry me?*** (Trad-arr. Hughes) Master Billy Neely B.B.C. Opera Orchestra. Cond. Stanford Robinson. Live off-air recording from Broadcasting House, London. Rec. 7/10/50. [0.54]

[21] **Birdsongs at Eventide*** (Barrie-Coates) Master Graham Payn Live performance 1932. [1.28]

[22] **Let the bright Seraphim** (Handel) Master Raymond Kinsey with orchestra Rec. 6/2/33. H.M.V. C. 2556 [4.46]

[23] **Angels guard thee** (Reilly-Godard) Master John Bonner with orchestra. Rec Christ Church Westminster Bridge Road. W.G. Webber, organ. Rec. Sept. 1929. Columbia DB 136 [2.41]

[24] **A song of wisdom*** (Charles V. Stanford) Master Beverley Jones Francis Jackson, organ York Minster. Private tape recording by John Rothera. Rec. 1954 [5.50]
TOTAL PLAYING TIME: 76.31
* Previously unissued material

THE BETTER LAND 5   AMPHION PHI CD 189

[1] **Rejoice Greatly** (Messiah - Handel) Master
Raymond Kinsey
Rec. 6/2/33. H.M.V. C. 2556 matrix 2B6269-1 [4.35]
[2] **Mighty like a rose** (Nevin-Staton) Master Michael
Morley John Mills - piano
Rec. 2/4/51. Decca LM 4543 (10 inch L.P.) matrices
DRL818-3b & CADPL817-1a [1.46]
[3] **If I can help somebody** (Androzzo) Master Michael
Morley Details as track 2 [2.55]
[4] **Hark! Hark! the lark** (Schubert) Master Ernest
Lough George Thalben-Ball - piano
Rec. 30/11/27. H.M.V. B. 2681 matrix Bb12074-2
[2.49]
[5] **There is a green hill far away** (Mrs C.F.
Alexander-Gounod) Master John Bonner
W Lloyd Weber - organ Rec. 9/1/29. Columbia 9832
matrix WAX4530-2 [3.43]
[6] **On Wings of Song** (England-Mendelssohn) Master
Thomas Criddle Andrew Fenner - piano Rec. 24/2/43.
H.M.V. BD 1046 matrix OEA 9973-1 [2.51]
[7] **Should he upbraid?** (Shakespeare-Sir Henry Bishop)
Master John Bonner with piano Rec. 8/1/29.
Columbia C 9840 matrix WAX 4527-2 [4.10]
[8] **Angels Serenade - La Seranata** (G. Braga) Master
John Bonner with orchestra & W. Lloyd Weber - organ
Rec. 9/1/29. Columbia 9832 matrix WAX 4529-1 [3.45]
[9] **Birdsong at Eventide** (Coates) Master Michael
Morley   Details as track 2, also issued as 78 r.p.m. disc
Decca M. 627 Matrix DR 16013-1 [2.56]
[10] **Y Deryn Pur -The Dove** (arr. Somervell-Williams)
Master Cyril Lewis Rec. 1934.
Decca F 5139 matrix TB1392-2 [2.37]
[11] **A song of long ago** (D. Furber-A.E. Adams)
MasterTrevor Schofield
Rec. 9/5/29. Columbia 5528 matrix A 8988-1 [2.59]
[12] **Nearer my God to Thee** (Carey)
 Master John Bookman Herbert Dawson - organ

11/7/34. H.M.V. test pressing matrix. Released
as H.M.V. B8241 matrix OB3587-2 [3.13]

[13] **A brown bird singing** (Barrie-Haydn Wood) Master
Leslie Day Rec. 22/6/33. Columbia DB 1147 [3.00]

[14] **Lullaby** (Brahms) Master Michael Morley Details
as track 2 [1.47]

[15] **O for the wings of a dove** (Mendelssohn) Master
Kenneth Purves Herbert Griffith - organ. Rec. 3/28. Stoll
Theatre, Kingsway. Broadcast 247 [3.10]

[16] **Father in Heaven*** (Largo-Handel)
Master Robert Regent James H. Lee - organ Rec.
19/1/38. Decca private recording, marix CP516 [2.53]

[17] **Hallelujah Exsultate Jubilate** (Mozart) Master
Billy Neely Gerald Moore - piano. Rec. Abbey Road
22/2/50. H.M.V. B. 10041 matrix OEA 14488-1 [3.00]

[18] **Abide with Me** (Liddle) Master Derek Barsham Fela
Sowande - organ Rec. Kingsway Hall, 1/11/44. Decca K.
1393 matrix AR 8816-2 [4.56]

[19] **Angels Ever bright** (Handel)
Master Robert Duncan Peel Rec. 21/9/27.
Columbia 9501 matrix WAX 3076-2 [2.57]

[20] **With Verdure Clad** (Creation-Haydn)
Master Raymond Kinsey
Rec. 24/4/33. H.M.V. C. 2571 matrix 2B6514-1 [4.35]

[21] **Oh for a closer walk with God** (Foster)
Master Raymond Kinsey Rec. 8/9/33.
H.M.V. C. 2629 matrix 2B3558-4 [4.02]

[22] **Beekeeper s Introit *** (arr. G. Dixon) Master
Alan Bradbrook Dr. George Thalben-Ball - organ of the
Temple Church. Private recording 1957 [0.56]

[23] **A song of peace*** (Charles V. Stanford)
Master Beverley Jones Francis Jackson - organ
Rec. 1954 York Minster. Private tape recording made by
the late John Rothera of York [5.28]

* Previously unissued material

TOTAL PLAYING TIME: 77.23

Due to the age and condition of some of these
recordings, levels of surface noise varies between
tracks

Recordings restored using the Cedar process, compiled & produced by Martin Monkman, Amphion Recordings

TEMPLE 1   AMPHION PHI CD 172

[1] **King of Glory** (Walford Davies) choir & organ. Rec. 15/4/27. H.M.V. B. 2493 [2.07]
[2] **I waited for the Lord** (Mendelssohn) Masters Ernest Lough & Ronald Mallett with choir and organ. Rec. 3/10/27. H.M.V. C. 1398 [4.12]
[3] **O come everyone that thirsteth** (Mendelssohn) Masters Ernest Lough & Ronald Mallett, Messrs Alfred Capel Dixon (tenor), Frank Hastwell (bass) with choir & organ. Rec. 14/7/27. H.M.V. C. 1398 [4.16]
[4] **How lovely are the Messengers** (Mendelssohn) choir & organ. Rec. 13/6/29. H.M.V. B. 3518 [3.11]
[5] **Lullay my liking** (Terry) Master Denis Barthel with choir, G.T.B. - piano &
  There is no rose (G.T.B.) Soloist A Capel
  Dixon, tenor. Unacc. with choir;
  [5] & [6] Rec. 25/9/31. H.M.V. B. 3976 [3.16]
[6] **See amid the winter s snow** (Goss) & **Christmas Lullab** (arr. G.T.B.) Unacc. with choir; Soloists Master Denis Barthel & A. Capel Dixon, tenor. Temple Church with Norman Greenwood - piano. [3.21]
[7] **O little town of Bethlehem** (Walford Davies), Master Denis Barthel acc. George Thalben-Ball. Rec. 24/3/32. H.M.V. B. 4285 [2.58]
[8] **As pants the hart** (Spohr) Master Thomas Meddings with choir & organ.
  Rec. 23/7/35. H.M.V. B. 8380 [3.11]
[9] **Lord it belongs not to my care** (Walford Davies) Unaccompanied, conducted by George Thalben-Ball. Rec. 13/6/30. H.M.V. B. 3518 [2.37]
[10] **Jesu joy of man's desiring** (J.S. Bach, arr.

Allen) Choir, piano & oboe (Leon Goossens).
Rec. 20/12/33. H.M.V. B. 8123 [2.37]
[11] **Blest are the departed** (Spohr) Master Thomas
Meddings with choir & organ.
Rec. 23/7/35. H.M.V. B. 8380 [3.03]
[12] **He was despised** (Handel) Master Denis Barthel
with organ. Rec. 24/2/32. H.M.V. B. 4107 [3.14]
[13] **Remember now thy Creator*** (Sterndale-Bennett)
Masters Harold Langston & Denis Barthel with
choir & organ. Rec. 3/7/30. Unpublished test pressing.
H.M.V. matrix BR2821-2 [3.18]
[14] **Oh for a closer walk with God*** (Spohr) Master
Harold Langston with choir & organ. Rec. 31/12/29.
Unpublished test pressing. H.M.V. matrix 2ER100-2 [4.26]
[15] **If ye love me, keep my commandments*** (Tallis)
Unaccompanied, directed by H. Walford Davies & assisted
by Mr. G.T. Ball. Rec. Hayes, 4/12/22. Unpublished test
pressing H.M.V. matrix Cc2239-2 (Acoustic recording)
[3.14]
[16] **O filii et filiae** (arr. Walford Davies) Masters
Ernest Lough & Douglas Horton with choir & organ. Rec.
15/4/27. H.M.V. B. 2493 [2.53]
[17] **Lord God of Heaven & Earth** (Spohr) Masters
Thomas Meddings & Dennys Lake
 with choir & organ. Rec. 20/12/33. H.M.V. B. 8123 [3.25]
[18] **Angels ever bright and fair*** (Handel) Master
Harold Langston with organ. Rec. 31/12/29. Unpublished
test pressing H.M.V. matrix BR 2712-2 [3.26]
[19] **Psalm 150** (Franck) Choir & organ. Rec. 25/9/31.
H.M.V. B. 4364 [2.59]
[20] **Hear my prayer** (Mendelssohn) Master Ernest Lough
with choir & organ. Rec. 30/3/28. H.M.V. C. 1329 [8.03]
[21] **The Heavens are telling** (Haydn-Creation) choir &
organ. Rec. 5/12/29. H.M.V. B. 2388 [5.17]
All tracks except those stated feature George Thalben-Ball
at the organ of the Temple Church
TOTAL PLAYING TIME: 77.18
* Previously unissued material

Temple Church Choir Recorded 1927-1932 Temple Church, London George Thalben-Ball - Organist & Director

[1] **Insanae et vanae curae** (Haydn). H.M.V. C. 2053. Rec.13/6/30. [6.55]

[2] **How lovely is Thy dwelling place**, from German Requiem (Brahms) H.M.V. test: BR 1959/60-1a. Rec.23/7/28. Published disc: B. 3453. [5.52]

[3] **Mine eyes have seen the Glory** (Walford Davies) H.M.V. test: BR 1165 1a. Rec. 3/10/27. Published disc: B. 2615. [2.37]

[4] **Hear ye, Israel** (part 1) (Mendelssohn) Master Ernest Lough Unpublised H.M.V. test. Rec. August 1927 [2.59]

[5] **O worship the King** (Tune: Old 104th)
       H.M.V. test: BR 2281-2. Rec. 14/2/29. Published disc B. 3047. [3.18]

[6] **Turn back O man** (Holst) H.M.V. B. 4364.   Rec. 3/7/30. [3.08]

[7] **For all the Saints** (Tune: Sine Nomine, Vaughan Williams) H.M.V. test: BR 11641. Rec.3/10/30. Published disc: B. 2615. [2.52]

[8] **St. Patrick's Prayer** (Burke) H.M.V. C. 1878. Rec. 4/3/30. [3.14]

[9] **Jerusalem** (Parry) Master Denis Barthel H.M.V. B. 4285. Rec. 24/2/32. [2.22]

[10] **Hallelujah from Christ at the Mount of Olives** (Beethoven) H.M.V. C. 1878. Rec. 4/3/30. [4.11]

[11] **Lead me, Lord** (Wesley) Soloists, Masters Ronald Mallett & Douglas Horton H.M.V. C. 1436. Rec. 14/7/27. [2.01]

[12] **Blessed be the God and Father** (Wesley)
       Soloists Masters Ernest Lough & Douglas Horton. H.M.V. C. 1541. Rec.21/2/28. [7.24] The Templars Male Voice Choir conducted by A. Capel Dixon Herbert Dawson - organ Recorded Abbey Road Studio One 21 September & 12 October 1948

[13] **God rest ye merry, Gentlemen** (Trad. arr. C. Dixon) H.M.V. C. 3806 [2.10]

[14] **A babe lies in the cradle** (Corner, arr. H.W.D./G.T-B) [2.33
H.M.V. test: 2EA 13277-4. Published disc: C. 3806.

[15] **Christ was born on Christmas Day** (Trad. adapted by H.W.D); H.M.V. C. 3806. [1.58]

[16] **While shepherds watched their flocks** (Winchester Old, arr. H.W.D.) [2.08]

[17] **Childing of a maiden** (Trad. arr. C. Dixon) [1.53] From E.M.I. master tape: 2EA 13274.

[18] **We three kings of Orient are** (J.H.Hopkins arr. C. Dixon) [2.32]

[19] **Christmas is coming / Wassail Carol** (Trad. arr. H.W.D.) [1.30] From E.M.I. master tape: 2EA 13275. [16]-[19] published disc: H.M.V. C. 3807.

The Templars directed by George Thalben-Ball - piano & organ   Recorded Abbey Road Studio One 2 October 1950

[20] **Away in a Manger** (Kirkpatrick arr. G.T.B.) [1.18]

[21] **The first Nowell** (Trad. arr. G.T.B.) From E.M.I. master tape: 2EA 15042. [2.09]

[22] **See amid the winter s snow** (Goss, arr. G.T.B.) E.M.I. master tape: 0EA 15046. [1.55]

[23] **Unto us a Boy is born** (Puer nobis nascitur arr. G.T.B.) [1.49]

[24] **Angels from the realms of Glory.** (Trad. French Carol arr. G.T.B.) [2.20] [23]-[24] from E.M.I. master tape: 2EA 15044.

[25] **O little town of Bethlehem** (Walford Davies arr. G.T.B.) [1.39] From E.M.I master tape: OEA 15046.

[26] **The Twelve days of Christmas** (Trad. arr. Frederic Austin) [3.1 Tenor soloist: Harry Abbott. Bass soloist: Ernest Lough. From E.M.I. master tape: OEA 15045.

[20]-[21] & [23]-[24] issued as H.M.V. C 4039. [22], [25] & [26] issued as H.M.V B. 9995.

[20]-[26] were also reissued on a 7 inch 45 r.p.m. extended play vinyl record: E.M.I. 7EG 7041.

All tracks originally released on 78 r.p.m. records. Tracks [16]-[26] are from E.M.I. master tapes.

The organ used in the 1948 & 1950 recordings was a Compton organ installed at Abbey Road in 1938
TOTAL PLAYING TIME: 78.02

TEMPLE CD 3   AMPHION PHI CD 210

[1] **The Lord God Omnipotent Reigneth** - George Thalben-Ball (1896-1987) [0.44]

[2] **Psalm 130 Chant in D minor, Psalm 48 Chant in E flat & Gloria Patri, Setting in E flat** - GeorgeThalben-Ball [5.24]

[3] **Te Deum Laudamus in E fla**t - Gerald Bullivant [7.45]

[4] **Jubilate Deo in B flat** - George Thalben-Ball [2.33]

[5] **The Greater Light** - Martin Shaw (1875-1958) [7.04]

[6] **When Jesus was born** (Christus) - Felix Mendelssohn (1809-1847) [6.56]

[7] **Flocks in Pastures Green abiding** - J.S. Bach (1685-1750) [5.08]

[8] **Nolo Mortem Peccatoris** - Thomas Morley (1557-1602) [3.18]

[9] **The Strife is O er** - Melchior Vulpius (c.1570-1615) arr. Henry Ley (1887-1962) [2.38]

[10] **He Was Despised** (Messiah) - George Frideric Handel (1685-1759)
Soloist: Martin Griffiths [4.42]

[11] **Doubt Not Thy Father s Care** - Edward Elgar (1857-1934) [2.56]

[12] **Kerygma** - Malcolm Williamson (1931-2003) [8.35]

[13] **Hymn of the Cherubim** - Sergei Rachmaninov (1873-1943) [3.39]

[14] **Splendente Te** - Wolfgang Amadeus Mozart

(1756-1791) [7.05]
[15] **Where Thou Reignest** - Franz Schubert (1797-1828)
[5.39]
[16] **Tarry No Longer** - Walford Davies (1869-1941) [1.38]
Soloists: Bass: William Johannes. Tenor: Richard Dawson.
Trebles: David Abbott, Richard Matthews, Martin Griffiths
& Ian le Grice. Recorded in the Temple Church, London.
Organist & Director of the Choir: Dr. George Thalben-Ball

[1]-[5], [7]-[9], [11], [15] & [16] recorded April
1977 and issued in 1979 as
L.P. record PVA 4917 545: Music from the Temple
Church. [13] & [14] from same sessions but
unpublished. Producer: Paul Vaughan. Recording
Engineers: Norman McLeod & David Welsby.
[12] From Abbey L.P. record HMP 2280: The Temple
Tradition. Recorded by Harry Mudd, 1980 reissued by
arrangement with Oxbridge Records
[6] Private recording 1960. [10] Private recording
1976.
Digitally remastered from master tapes & produced by
Martin Monkman, Amphion Recordings, 2004.
TOTAL PLAYING TIME: 77.26

Patrons

Douglas Brooks-Davies, Cheadle, Cheshire

James Dyer, Luton

Dr. Roy Massey MBE, Tewkesbury, Gloucestershire

James and Mary Probetts, Talbot House, Wimbledon

Ian Day Adams, Kennington, London

Peter Ward, Nightingale Square, London

Norman Wilkinson, Wilmslow, Chesire

John Russell, Lytchette Matravers, Dorset

James and Mary Probetts, Talbot House, Wimbledon

Bernard Haunch, Sutton, Surrey

Philip Hilstrop, Cromer, Norfolk

Nicholas Wilton, Thornton Heath, Surrey

Vincent McDonnell, Tullamore, Co. Offaly

Dr. Andrew Plant

Michel Smith, Presteigne, Powys

Dennis Young, Clifton, York

Philip Woods, Pinner, Middlesex

Douglas R. Carrington, Lytham St. Annes

Mr. J. R. Lester, Ravenshead, Nottingham

Sylvia M. Cross (Miss), Headington, Oxford

Mr. H. Paling, Northhants

David J. Herschell, Dunblane, Perthshire

Mr. A. C. Hales, Frinton-on-Sea, Essex

John Nias, Holloway, London

Mrs. Jill E. Staplehurst, Bury St. Edmunds, Suffolk

Gordon L. Ridgard, Preston Candover, Hants

S.A. Old, Walton, Liverpool

Stephen Rhode, San Diego, California

Dr. Dennis Townhill O.B.E., Edinburgh

Edwinna Marshall, Loma Linda, California

Mrs. Susan Brazier, Chelmsford, Essex

Christopher Morris, Paoli, Pennsylvania

Mrs. Denise Morris, Carlisle, Cumbria

Mr. A.J. Thomas, Eastbourne, East Sussex

David H. Hunt, Denver, Pennsylvania

R.A. Bawden, Mill Hill, London

Mr. D.A. Edward, Yeovil

Marius Oliver, Punerot, France

Cherry Johnstone, Canterbury, Kent

Frederick Appleby, Lonsdale Road, London

Peter Hopper, Scunthorpe

J.W. Reid, Okehampton, Devon

R.J. Pugh, Pontypridd, Wales

Brian Barry, Ryhope, Sunderland

Mr. Gary H. Geivet, Kernville, California

Major Denis Barthel, Vancouver, British Columbia

Mr. Graham Trew, Knighton, Powys

Mr. J.I. Mitchell, High Wycombe, Bucks

Everson Whittle, Bolton, Lancs

Graham Butcher, Mansfield, Nottingham

Mrs. D. Brookman, Beckenham, Kent

Mr. David Dimmock, Exeter, New Hampshire USA.

Mr. Robert Coates, HarØy, Norway.

Mr. Bruce W. Cameron, Glasgow

David Nicholas, Eastdon, Devon

Dr. Sander Bergman, West Hills, California

Alvin Clement, Belmont Hills, New Zealand

Dr. John T. Dizer, Utica, New York

Pascal Moré, Karlsruhe, Germany

Dr. Bruce Rye, Dallas Texas

Ricky Wilkinson, Westhorpe, Suffolk

Mark Ervin,Valley Lee, Maryland, U.S.A.

Mr. Lynn Scoch, Bloomington, Indiana

Mr. Frank Edmonds, Alpha Records Ltd., London

William E. Ferguson, Leigh, Lancashire

Ross Cozens, Strongsville Ohio, U.S.A.

Stuart W. Grigg, Grosse Pointe, Missouri, U.S.A.

Alvin Clement, Lower Hutt, New Zealand

Malcolm and Eileen Creese, Romsey, Hampshire

Dudley Green, Clitheroe, Lancashire

Adrian Smith, Chelmsford, Essex

June Farrar, King's Road, Belfast

Peter Joelson, Surbiton, Surrey

Margaret Fox, University of Wales Swansea

Kathryn West, Swansea

John Moulton, Christchurch, New Zealand

William Wainwright, Sheffield

Mr. Raymond Quinn, Bangor, Northern Ireland

Mark Newton, St. Lucia, QLD Australia

J. E. J. P. B. Bishop-Guest, Romford, Essex

Andrew Zalewski, New Cross, London

Barry Cutler, Beckenham, Kent

Robert Harris, Goostrey, Cheshire

R. A. Bawden, Mill Hill, London

Dr. Maurice Merrell, London W19 4LG

Mrs. B. M. Carter, Mickle Trafford, Cheshire

Peter Kruger, Indoorphilly, Queensland, Australia.